New Forest National Park draft boundary

Public consultation report

Distributed by:
Countryside Agency Publications
PO Box 125
Wetherby
West Yorkshire LS23 7EP

Telephone   0870 120 6466
Fax   0870 120 6467
website   www.countryside.gov.uk
Minicom   0870 120 7405 (for the hard of hearing)

Contents

Foreword

The Countryside Agency (and its predecessor the Countryside Commission) have been involved in caring for the New Forest for some 30 years and during this time have kept its conservation needs under review. National, regional and local changes are beginning to put pressure on the Forest and diminish its natural beauty, tranquillity and way of life.

We believe that designation as a National Park is the best way to address these changes in ways that will meet the needs of the New Forest. But we are clear that a National Park Authority must reflect the special circumstances of the Forest. These include existing bodies with statutory responsibilities, the Forest's special legislation, the importance of commoning, and the area's high nature conservation value. Within the basic framework, each English National Park Authority is different, with members, policies and activities to meet its own particular needs. We want to use this flexibility to find the right solution for the unique area that is the New Forest.

A National Park Authority would have specific purposes, wide reaching powers and dedicated resources to conserve and enhance the area, and to help people understand and enjoy it. It would act as a champion for the Forest – locally, nationally and internationally. Existing bodies in the Forest can, and do, act to address many of the issues facing the Forest. As in other National Parks, a New Forest National Park Authority would work in partnership with the existing bodies, responding to opportunities creatively and doing things they cannot do. National Park designation would not repeal or amend the New Forest Acts, and would not change the powers of the Verderers or the Forestry Commission.

We have two tasks: to identify a boundary for the proposed National Park and to prepare advice to Government on the arrangements needed for a New Forest National Park Authority if a National Park designation is ultimately confirmed by the Secretary of State.

This document sets out our initial thoughts on where the National Park boundary should be, based on the criteria set out in legislation. We are circulating it and a consultation leaflet very widely within and around the Forest. We have allowed plenty of time for people to respond and we want to hear from as many people as possible. We will consider every response we get very carefully.

We are working in parallel on the second task of developing proposed arrangements to reflect the special needs of the Forest. We will consult on these early next year.

I look forward to hearing your views about the boundary we propose.

Ewen Cameron
Chairman

New Forest National Park draft boundary: public consultation report

Errata

P62 Map

- Dibden Purleigh near A326: amend to Dibden Purlieu

Map at back of document

- A35 at Everton: amend to A337
- Exbury on B3054: amend to Beaulieu
- Dibden Purleigh near A326: amend to Dibden Purlieu
- Normansland near B3089: amend to Nomansland

1 Introduction

The Countryside Agency (and the Countryside Commission before it) has long considered that the New Forest merits National Park status. We believe that making this much-loved and valuable area a National Park is the best way to meet its conservation needs.

One of the priorities is to define the National Park area. The first stage of this is to identify a draft New Forest National Park boundary and seek views on it. That is the purpose of this document.

The New Forest is important because it is a remarkable historic landscape – the most intact survival of a medieval hunting and pastoral system in England, perhaps even in Europe. It is a unique landscape, with a distinctive combination of woodland, grass lawns and the largest extent of lowland heath in Britain.

Many factors, both human and natural, have shaped the landscape of the New Forest. The traditional system of land management known as commoning has been particularly important in creating and maintaining its landscape and distinctive wildlife. Commoning as a way of life is also a key element of the cultural heritage, economy and community life of the area.

The New Forest is also very important for recreation, with the Crown land (managed by the Forestry Commission) offering extensive open access. In addition there are many footpaths and bridleways as well as a wide range of visitor attractions and opportunities for people to enjoy the Forest's wildlife and history.

National Park status will give the New Forest the best possible protection and management because there will be a permanent designation and a dedicated body – a National Park Authority – whose whole purpose will be to care for the area. The Authority will have special powers and substantial resources to achieve this.

In 1998 the Countryside Commission recommended to the Government that the New Forest be formally designated as a National Park[1]. It suggested doing this through tailor-made legislation because of the special circumstances in the New Forest. However, if such legislation was not possible, then designation of the New Forest as a National Park would be justified against the criteria of the existing National Park legislation and would meet the Forest's needs.

In September 1999 the Government decided that special legislation was not possible. It asked the Countryside Agency to consider designating the New Forest as a National Park under the existing legislation[2]. In October 1999 the Agency decided to begin the process of creating a New Forest National Park.

1. Countryside Commission, Advice to Government on Protected Areas (CCP 532), Countryside Commission, 1998.

2. Letter to the Countryside Agency from the Rt Hon Michael Meacher, Minister for the Environment, 29 September, 1999.

Outline of the draft boundary

- In the East (Totton and the waterside) it follows a line similar to that of the New Forest Heritage Area. The principal differences are extensions at Totton, Dibden and Calshot, where the Heritage Area meets the AONB.

- In the South it follows the low water mark from Calshot Point to Hurst Beach at Keyhaven, taking in the whole of the Solent Coast and waterfront, including all of the South Hampshire AONB and Lymington.

- In the West it includes most of the Avon valley, but excludes Ringwood and the extensive areas of modern development north of Fordingbridge.

- In the North – Wiltshire and the Test valley – it is the same as the existing Heritage Area.

See Map A and Chapters 5 and 6 which give more details.

3. Environmental Resources Management, New Forest National Park Boundary Study, July 2000.

4. The New Forest Heritage Area has planning policies as if it were a National Park. Its boundary is defined through the local plan process and may be reviewed and amended when local plans are reviewed.

Defining the National Park boundary

The Countryside Agency has identified the draft boundary which is set out in this document, drawing on a technical study commissioned from consultants Environmental Resources Management (ERM)[3].

The proposed boundary includes all of the New Forest Heritage Area[4] and also much of the Avon valley, the whole of the Solent Coast and the rest of the South Hampshire Area of Outstanding Natural Beauty (AONB), and land alongside Southampton Water not currently in the Heritage Area.

This report sets out in full the Agency's initial proposals for a National Park boundary. It explains that National Park boundaries need to be based on the statutory criteria set out in legislation – natural beauty and opportunities for open-air recreation. It also describes the factors that the Countryside Agency (which has statutory responsibility for designating National Parks) takes into account in drawing the boundary.

The report explains why we have included certain areas. It also explains why we have not included other areas. The maps at the back of the report (maps 1–20) show the detailed line of the draft boundary.

We want your views

The boundary identified in this document is a draft. We now want to hear from everybody (individuals, local authorities and other organisations) with a view: whether, on the basis of National Park criteria and the detailed boundary considerations set out in this report (see Chapter 2), they think the proposed boundary is right and, if not, how it should be changed and why. We will look very carefully at the **reasons** people give for their views, which need to relate to the statutory criteria and policy for National Parks and detailed boundary considerations.

We are consulting widely to ensure that the final boundary is best for the future of the New Forest. We will consider very carefully all the comments we receive. We will then publish a formal draft boundary and consult the local authorities (as the legislation requires) in 2001. We will consider the local authority responses and decide whether any further changes are needed before preparing a National Park Designation Order to submit to the Secretary of State for the Environment, Transport and the Regions in late 2001.

How to make your views known
Format for comments

We specifically need to know whether you agree with the boundary we have proposed or whether you think it should be changed. In either case, please give your reasons.

We have divided the boundary into 17 sections to make it easier for you to respond and for us to consider your comments. Map A shows all 17 sections of the boundary. There are also more detailed maps at the back (Maps 1

Boundary sections

1. North of Totton
2. Totton Bypass
3. Eling
4. Marchwood
5. Dibden Bay
6. Hythe to Langley
7. Langley to Fawley
8. Ashlett Creek
9. Calshot
10. Solent Coast
11. Lymington River to Everton
12. Everton to Highcliffe
13. Avon valley: below Ringwood (and boundary excluding Ringwood)
14. Avon valley: Ringwood to Fordingbridge
15. Avon valley: North of Fordingbridge
16. Searchfield Farm to Plaitford Green
17. Plaitford Green to A3090

to 20), showing each section (see left).

You may want to comment on more than one section. Please make it clear to which section(s) your comments apply by using the boundary section numbers above.

You may want to look in particular at those sections where there are major changes to the Heritage Area boundary (see Chapter 4 of this document). These are:

• land north of Totton, including part of the M27 corridor (boundary section 1)

• Dibden Bay (boundary section 5)

• Calshot (boundary section 9)

• Lymington (boundary section 11)

• the Avon valley south of Ringwood (boundary section 13)

• the Avon valley between Ringwood and Fordingbridge (boundary section 14).

In all cases, whether you agree with our draft boundary or wish to propose a change, it is important that you explain your reasons. Please set these out as clearly as possible. It is very important your reasons relate to:
a) the statutory criteria for the designation of National Parks, which are:

• **their natural beauty**
• **the opportunities they afford for open-air recreation and/or**

b) the Countryside Agency's detailed boundary considerations set out in Chapter 2 of this document.

We will not be able to take responses fully into account unless they relate to these statutory criteria. Chapter 6 shows how we interpreted them in arriving at the draft boundary. You may wish to comment particularly on these points.

If you wish to propose an amendment to any part of the boundary, please describe the alternative line you suggest in sufficient detail so that it can be marked on a map. A copy of a map showing your suggestions would be ideal.

We have also produced a consultation leaflet which will be made widely available throughout the area and beyond. This asks the same questions and includes a pro forma for responses which you may wish to use. Copies are available from Countryside Agency Publications, PO Box 125, Wetherby, West Yorkshire LS23 7EP. Tel: 0870 120 6466 Fax: 0870 120 6467

Where and when to send comments

Please send your comments to: New Forest Boundary Consultation, PO Box 33206, London, SW1H 0WP

or by email via the Countryside Agency's website: **www.countryside.gov.uk** as soon as possible, but to arrive not later than **19 January 2001.**

If you have any queries please telephone the 24–hour answerphone service on **020 7340 2982**

2 National Parks

The Countryside Agency is responsible for designating National Parks. The statutory status of National Park provides the highest degree of protection for the most beautiful expanses of country in England where people can enjoy a wide range of open air recreation. England's eight National Parks (including the Broads) are part of a world-wide network of protected areas.

National Parks are designated under the National Parks and Access to the Countryside Act 1949 (amended by the Countryside Act 1968 and the Environment Act 1995). Appendix A gives details of the legislation.

Defining a National Park boundary

The New Forest National Park boundary will have to meet the criteria for National Parks set out in the 1949 Act, as interpreted by Countryside Agency policy. It will also need to take into account the Countryside Agency's agreed approach to drawing the detailed boundary of a National Park.

National Park criteria

The 1949 Act defines National Parks as extensive tracts of country in England and Wales designated because of:

"(a) their natural beauty, and

(b) the opportunities they afford for open-air recreation, having regard both to their character and to their position in relation to centres of population".

In February 2000 the Countryside Agency Board agreed a new policy for applying these criteria in the light of modern requirements[5]. It agreed that the key issue to be considered in designating new National Parks (other than natural beauty) is whether the area is capable of providing a markedly superior recreational experience.

How the criteria were interpreted to draft the New Forest boundary

The statutory criteria have been the main point of reference in identifying the draft boundary. The approach taken is that all areas included should meet both of these criteria, in varying degrees.

Table 1 explains how the statutory criteria of natural beauty and opportunities for open-air recreation have been interpreted in identifying a draft boundary, taking account of legislation and new Countryside Agency thinking on its approach to designating National Parks.

The natural beauty criterion encompasses both the considerations that were used to identify boundaries for the New Forest Heritage Area – natural beauty and essential grazing land. The principal 'additional' criterion used in identifying a National Park boundary is opportunities for open-air recreation.

The core area of the New Forest meets both these criteria very fully. The key question is how far the

5. Countryside Agency, National Park Designation: A review of how the criteria are applied, Board paper, February 2000 (AP 00/03).

area of national importance for natural beauty and recreation extends.

Drawing a National Park boundary in detail

The Countryside Agency has also reviewed its approach to drawing the detailed boundary of a National Park.

The Agency's approach is based closely on that set out in the 1947 Report of the National Parks Committee – known as the Hobhouse Report[6] (see Appendix A). The Hobhouse approach was used for defining National Park boundaries in the 1950s and for subsequent boundary reviews.

The Agency agreed its new approach (see Table 2) in July 2000. This new approach was used in identifying a draft boundary for the New Forest National Park.

Table 1.
Interpretation of statutory criteria for National Park designation

Criterion	Interpretation
Natural beauty	• Natural beauty implies a landscape of outstanding national or international importance.
	• It is defined to embrace flora, fauna, geological and physiographical features. Archaeological, historical, cultural, architectural and vernacular features are also included (in accordance with guidance and precedent).
	• A key concept is that of landscape quality. This is a function of distinctive character, presence of key characteristics, absence of atypical and incongruous features, and the state of repair of the landscape, as well as how intact it is.
	• Visual, intangible, ecological, historical and cultural characteristics, features and values are all relevant to natural beauty and landscape quality.
	• In the New Forest, the historic dispersed pastoral system is a key cultural characteristic that created and helps to maintain New Forest character, and as such should be taken into account in designation.
Opportunities afforded for a markedly superior recreational experience, having regard both to character and position in relation to centres of population	• The National Park should provide an extensive tract of countryside, of sufficient size to offer opportunities for open-air recreation for large numbers of people.
	• There should be (existing and/or potential) scope to provide a markedly superior recreational experience, of national importance.
	• Opportunities for understanding and enjoying the area's special qualities (ie. its landscape character and quality) are particularly relevant.
	• Land within the National Park should be suitable for quiet enjoyment, particularly walking (therefore open access and public rights of way are relevant) and other appropriate activities eg. riding, boating.
	• General accessibility, catchment area, ease of travel (especially by public transport) should be taken into account, as well as openness and remoteness where appropriate.

6. The National Parks Committee, Report of the National Parks Committee (England and Wales), HMSO, 1947.

Table 2.
The Countryside Agency's approach to defining National Park boundaries

1. The Countryside Agency shall first determine in broad terms that an area of land meets the statutory criteria for designation.
2. It shall then in drawing a National Park boundary take account together of the following considerations.
   a. Areas of high landscape quality should be included within the area of land identified for designation.
   b. Areas to be included may be of differing landscape character: quality will be the key determinant rather than uniformity.
   c. Areas which provide or are capable of providing a markedly superior recreational experience should be included.
   d. Boundaries should include land and settlements which contribute to the rural economy and community life within the Park and to the Park's special qualities and purposes. Such areas should however be excluded where activities there, in particular urban or industrial development, conflict with or outweigh the essential values of the Park.
   e. Wherever possible, an easily distinguishable physical boundary should be chosen.
   f. Where local government boundaries follow suitable lines, it may be administratively convenient to adopt them. In the majority of cases, however, they will be unsuitable.
   g. Towns or villages should not normally be cut in two by a National Park boundary: inclusion or exclusion should normally depend on their contribution as a whole to the character and purposes of the Park.
   h. Unsightly development on the edge of a National Park should generally be excluded, although the possibility of its modification or screening should not be overlooked where the immediately surrounding country claims inclusion.
   i. Land allocated in adopted development plans as to be worked for the quarrying and mining of important deposits on the margins of a National Park should normally be excluded from the Park, unless the land will be restored to a land use and quality which contributes to Park purposes. This approach will also apply to major industrial and commercial developments for which land is allocated in adopted development plans at the time of designation.
   j. Features of scientific, historic or architectural value (eg. Nature Reserves, important archaeological sites and Ancient Monuments) which are situated on the margins of a National Park should be included where practicable.
3. The statutory criteria point to the inclusion of land where both high landscape quality and a markedly superior recreational opportunity exist. Not all land within the Park must necessarily satisfy both criteria (a) and (c), but there should be a high degree of concurrence.
4. The boundary should not be regarded as a sharp barrier between areas of differing quality. In most situations there will be a transition of landscape quality and recreational experience across a sweep of land: the boundary chosen should be an easily identifiable feature within this transition.

Explanatory notes
1. The criteria are defined in S5(2) in the 1949 National Parks and Access to the Countryside Act and shall be applied according to the Agency's policy adopted in February 2000.
2a. Landscape quality includes visual and intangible features and values. It embraces natural beauty, wildlife and cultural heritage. It is interpreted as the extent to which the landscape demonstrates the presence of key characteristics and the absence of atypical or incongruous ones, and by its state of repair and integrity. This is in line with the Countryside Agency's approach to landscape assessment.
2b. A variety of landscape character is an important factor in the overall amenity of the Park. Usually however there will be some unifying factors, such as land use, ecosystems, historical or cultural links which bring differing character areas together to be included in a National Park.
2c. Recreation means quiet countryside recreation related to the character of the area: that which allows people to enjoy and understand the special qualities of the Park, without damaging it or conflicting with its purposes or spoiling the enjoyment of it by others. This definition can encompass a number of different activities.
2e. This is both for administrative reasons and for the convenience of the visiting public. Roads and railways frequently provide such a boundary.
2f. Local government boundaries are usually unsuitable because they follow no defined physical feature, may be subject to alteration and seldom conform to the limits of landscape quality or recreational value.
2g. This may include a contribution to the Park's economy and community life, and a value for visitors; eg. provision of accommodation, access to public transport, information or other services.
3. This approach is in line with the Agency's policy for designation, adopted in February 2000.

3 The New Forest

The New Forest lies mainly in south-west Hampshire. Broadly, it extends from the Avon valley in the west to Southampton Water in the east, and from the Solent Coast in the south to the edge of the Wiltshire chalk downs in the north. Fashioned by centuries of human use and intervention, it is an area of outstanding landscape, wildlife and historic interest. Part of the Forest is defined as Heritage Area and the South Hampshire coast is designated as an AONB.

The designation history of the area is outlined in Appendix B.

The New Forest and the National Park criteria

In order to identify a draft boundary for the New Forest, each potential area has been assessed in terms of its natural beauty and the opportunities it offers for recreation: the two National Park criteria.

Because the importance of core areas of the Forest is widely acknowledged, particular attention has been given to the marginal areas to see if they meet National Park criteria and therefore should be included within the National Park.

Natural beauty

The character and quality of the land at the heart of the New Forest, within the current perambulation (the historic term for the boundary of the area governed by Forest law), are described very fully in The New Forest Landscape, CCP 220[7] and a number of other sources. That report gives the following principal reasons why the area is widely recognised as having 'natural beauty'.

- **It is an outstanding historic landscape**
  It is a remarkable survival of a medieval hunting forest and pastoral system, although the origins of this form of land management are much earlier. It is the most intact example in England, perhaps even in Europe. In addition, it is of prime cultural importance as the only Royal Forest where traditional ownership and practices – Forest law administered by the Court of Verderers – survive.

- **It is a landscape with a unique character**
  It includes not only the largest extent of heathland in lowland Britain but also an intimate mix of a distinctive set of landscape types. The Forest is a mosaic of old woodland, managed forestry inclosures, extensive tracts of heathland with boggy ground, grass lawns and enclosed areas of farmland and villages. The different types of landscape are clearly linked historically and through their present-day functions.

7. Countryside Commission, The New Forest Landscape. (CCP 220), Countryside Commission, 1986.

- **It is a landscape with aesthetic appeal**

  The New Forest has long been a source of inspiration for writers, artists and photographers whose work has helped to shape other people's image of the Forest. The picturesque qualities of the landscape are seen as being particularly English, even an image of 'ideal' countryside.

In defining a draft boundary, natural beauty has been considered in terms of landscape, ecology, history and commoning.

Landscape considerations

'Natural beauty' is inextricably bound up with landscape character, that is the pattern of elements that occurs consistently in a certain type of landscape. Each landscape is made distinctive by its own particular combination of characteristics and features. These same qualities are relevant in judging the importance and value of the landscape. This is especially true in the New Forest, where natural beauty is closely related to the particular range of landscape types.

The landscape types on which the draft New Forest National Park boundary are based are taken from the New Forest District Landscape Character Assessment[8] (see Table 7 in Appendix D). The character and quality of the New Forest landscapes are explained fully in Appendix D.

All the typical New Forest landscapes fall within the New Forest Countryside Character Area[9] and share a number of key characteristics:

- historically they were an integral part of the New Forest system of land management, with its complex mosaic of woodland, heathland, grassland and farmland landscapes;
- they have ancient features – not only woodland, heathland, ancient enclosures and settlements, but also ancient drove roads that link the enclosed landscapes to the adjoining open forest;
- they are still characterised by commoning influences, including grazing animals, and the associated traditional smallholdings.

These landscapes also differ from those of adjoining areas. To the east, the South Hampshire Lowlands Countryside Character Area is a mainly pastoral landscape of small, irregular fields and woodlands on rich deep soils. To the west, the Dorset Heaths Character Area shares a similar geology to the New Forest, but is a larger-scale, more sparsely populated landscape with extensive conifer plantations. To the north, the Salisbury Plain and the West Wiltshire Downs Character Area is an extensive, open, rolling chalk plateau dominated by large arable fields.

The key characteristics and features of each of the principal types of landscape are described in Appendix D. These provide a yardstick for judging the quality of a landscape and whether it should be included within the National Park. The obvious types of

8. Environmental Resources Management, New Forest District Landscape Character Assessment, report to New Forest District Council, Hampshire County Council, The Countryside Agency and English Heritage, 2000.

9. Countryside Agency, Countryside Character Volume 7, The South East and London (CA 13), Countryside Agency, 1999

landscape to consider for inclusion are the river terrace farmlands and river floodplain of the Avon valley, plus parts of the coastal fringe and coastal plain estates.

Key questions to ask about these areas include:

- how distinctive is the landscape character of the area?
- how much does the area demonstrate the key characteristics of a particular type of landscape?
- is the landscape in good condition?
- are there clear visual and/or functional links to other parts of the Forest?
- are there intangible landscape qualities, such as wilderness or a sense of tranquillity, that may be highly valued?

These issues are considered in detail for each area in Chapters 5 and 6.

In addition, it is important to consider the ecological, historical and land management characteristics and features that contribute to landscape character, quality and natural beauty.

Ecological considerations

The nature conservation character and interest of the area looked at is described in the New Forest Natural Area Profile[10]. This supports the idea of a broad definition of New Forest landscapes, encompassing not only the Crown land – the core – but also the coast and the Avon valley.

The ecology of the New Forest habitat types and the key features

of nature conservation interest are described in Appendix D.

Significant areas are of European and international importance for nature conservation under the EC Habitat and Birds Directives and the Ramsar International Convention for the Protection of Wetlands.

- Because it includes a mosaic of habitats and species that are threatened in a European context, the New Forest core is a candidate Special Area of Conservation (cSAC), a Special Protection Area (SPA) and a Ramsar site.
- Much of the Solent and Southampton Water are designated as a candidate SAC, an SPA and a Ramsar site because of their coastal habitats and importance for birds.
- The Avon valley from Christchurch to Bickerton, which includes a wide range of river valley and wetland habitats and is important for breeding and wintering birds, is designated as an SPA and a Ramsar site. The river is also a candidate SAC throughout its full length.

In addition to these designations there are several Sites of Special Scientific Interest (SSSIs) that are of national nature conservation importance. The whole river floodplain extending north into Wiltshire is also part of the Avon Valley Environmentally Sensitive Area (ESA).

Both the habitat character and the distribution of sites of nature

10. English Nature Hampshire and Isle of Wight Team, New Forest Natural Area Profile, English Nature, 1998.

conservation interest have influenced the draft boundary. In accordance with the Agency's approach to defining National Park boundaries (Table 2), wherever practicable the draft boundary includes features of nature conservation importance which are on the margins of the National Park.

Historical considerations

The area's archaeological, historical, cultural, architectural and vernacular character and quality are all relevant considerations in identifying a National Park boundary. The historic landscape character of the New Forest is described in the New Forest Landscape Character Assessment[11], the Hampshire Historic Landscape Assessment[12], and the New Forest Archaeological/Historical Landscape Character Assessment[13].

The history of human settlement in the New Forest dates back at least to the Bronze Age when the land was largely cleared of its primeval forest, becoming infertile and able to support only heathland. On pockets of richer soils within the Forest and all around the edge, ancient woodland survived and settled farming communities were established by local woodland clearance, a process known as assarting. The Royal Hunting Forest, established in 1079, formalised this situation. Key elements have survived to the present day in the form of rights of common, which allow the surrounding communities access to Forest resources. The Court of Verderers administers the commoning system.

These basic historic landscape patterns, which have been in place for a thousand years or more, are still reflected in today's landscape. They are described in Appendix D.

The unique historical and cultural status of the New Forest is widely recognised. The UK Government has proposed to the World Heritage Convention that the Forest should be a World Heritage Site on the grounds that it is an area of outstanding wildlife and landscape interest, fashioned by human intervention and use over thousands of years. The proposed World Heritage site description[14] refers to the area's rich archaeological heritage, particularly Bronze Age and Roman, and its documented history which goes back to the 11th century.

Formal common rights were established by the mid 16th century. The quality of the habitats and landscapes of the New Forest is widely acknowledged as being dependent on the exercise of common rights and the continued existence of a small community of active commoners who make up a distinct social group. The visual and historical continuity and the shared history of the Forest core and the more fertile areas around the periphery are highlighted as key historical and cultural qualities of the area.

The area includes many Scheduled Ancient Monuments, sites shown on the English

11. Environmental Resources Management, New Forest District Landscape Character Assessment, report to New Forest District Council, Hampshire County Council, The Countryside Agency and English Heritage, 2000.

12. Oxford Archaeological Unit and Scott Wilson, Hampshire Historic Landscape Assessment, report to Hampshire County Council and English Heritage, 1999.

13. Wessex Archaeology, The New Forest Archaeological/Historical Landscape Character Assessment, report to the New Forest Committee, 1996.

14. Department for Culture, Media and Sport, World Heritage Sites: The Tentative List of the United Kingdom of Great Britain and Northern Ireland, Department for Culture, Media and Sport, 1999.

Heritage Register of Historic Parks and Gardens, and Conservation Areas (all designations of national importance)[15]. There are also many other sites of archaeological, historical and architectural interest. Where practicable, important sites around the margins of the area have been included within the draft National Park boundary. This has influenced the line, particularly south of Lymington and in the Avon valley where there are a number of Conservation Areas.

Commoning considerations

The traditional commoning system of land management remains a key feature of the New Forest's rural economy and community life. It is also of crucial importance to the landscape and ecological character of the Forest and to the continuance of that character[16]. Commoning has therefore been an important consideration in identifying a draft boundary.

Land with rights to forest and common grazing occurs both within the Forest perambulation and in the broad fringe of countryside around the periphery, extending fairly continuously along the waterside, the Solent Coast and the Avon valley, as well as northwards into Wiltshire[17]. The rights are definitive, attached to the landholding, and cannot be extinguished even if they are not exercised.

Commoners are individuals who exercise Forest and/or common rights. They exercise their grazing rights by turning their stock on to the open forest (depasturing). Only a small number are able to make a complete living from commoning; most are part-time commoners supplementing their income from other sources. Others simply keep one or two animals on the Forest to maintain this age-old tradition.

It helps if commoners have access to 'backup grazing'[18] to support their commoning activities. This land may be owned or rented. In recent years commoners have found it increasingly difficult to purchase suitable properties and small holdings because of very high prices – reflecting the area's popularity with commuters and holidaymakers. In addition, it has become very difficult to purchase or rent suitable paddocks or fields because of the premium values of such land for more intensive forms of agriculture, recreational horse-keeping and, in some cases, mineral extraction and urban development.

Against this background, and in order to assess the way in which commoning considerations should influence the National Park boundary, a review was carried out as part of the boundary study the Agency commissioned[19]. It looked at the current status of the commoning system, trends over the last 30 years, and backup grazing. The findings of the review are described in Appendix D.

A key issue in drafting a boundary was how to take account of the long-term needs

15. Data provided by local authorities.

16. Further information on the commoning system and its evolution can be found in Countryside Commission, The New Forest Commoners (CCP 164), Countryside Commission, 1984 and Stagg, D and J Page, Two Reports on New Forest Commoning (CCD 45), Countryside Commission, 1989.

17. Stagg, D and Page, J. Two Reports on New Forest Commoning (CCD 45), Countryside Commission, 1989.

18. 'Backup grazing' is the enclosed pasture land that supports use of the Forest for common grazing. Generally it is located close to a commoner's holding. Its uses include overwintering stock, raising store cattle, making hay or silage, tending sick animals and young stock, and preparing stock for market. In addition to the land that is in use as backup grazing at present, there is a wider pool of land currently used for other purposes that might be capable of use as backup grazing for future generations of commoners, subject to availability and cost.

19. Specialist input to the study in relation to commoning and backup grazing was provided by Joanne Way (nee Page). The full findings are presented in two working papers submitted to the Countryside Agency.

and sustainability of the commoning system. The principal aim was to include within the National Park an adequate supply of land (affordable for commoners to own or rent) which could serve as backup grazing. A secondary consideration was to include areas that were formerly grazed in conjunction with the open forest.

Because there has been lengthy – and often inconclusive – debate in the past about the definition of an adequate supply of backup grazing, ERM carried out qualitative desk research and structured interviews with key people in the Forest with personal knowledge and experience of commoning and grazing issues (see Appendix D). The findings of this work were also used to help identify a draft National Park boundary.

Opportunities for open-air recreation

It is widely recognised that the New Forest meets the second statutory criterion for designation as a National Park – outstanding opportunities for open-air recreation. The area is renowned for the opportunities there are to enjoy its landscape, and its special qualities attract a high number of visitors.

Walkers are able to enjoy the open forest through the accepted privilege of access to enjoy 'air and exercise' on Crown Land[20].

The South Hampshire AONB is also of considerable recreational importance. The Solent Coast is internationally recognised for sailing and boating. It is the longest stretch of unspoilt coastline on England's south-east coast.

Many visitors are attracted to the

New Forest because it is one of the few remaining extensive quiet rural areas in the crowded and highly urbanised south-east of England. Research by the University of Portsmouth[21] shows that the top four reasons for visiting the New Forest are scenery, ease of access, peace and quiet, and to see the ponies and cattle.

The most recent estimates indicate that the New Forest receives in the region of 7 million day visits per year[22]. However, research by the University of Portsmouth in 1996 has shown that this figure may underestimate the number of visits to the Forest made by local people (possibly accounting for up to 18 million per year)[23].

Around 40 per cent of visits are by holidaymakers; 30 per cent by local residents; and 30 per cent by day visitors from elsewhere[24].

The New Forest fulfils a particular role for local communities in the waterside parishes and the southern coastal towns. The majority of the area's day visitors come from Southampton and Bournemouth/ Poole. It is estimated that 15 million people live within day trip range.

One of the greatest challenges is to make sure that the very things people have come to enjoy are conserved. This means both improving the management of existing recreational resources, developing new opportunities for quiet, open-air recreation, and managing the area – Forest core, coast and peripheral landscapes – as a whole. The area proposed may offer new opportunities to alleviate recreational pressures on the Forest core.

Recreational use of the Forest is described more fully in Appendix E.

20. Countryside Commission, The New Forest Landscape (CCP 220), Countryside Commission, 1986.

21. Land Management Research Unit of the University of Portsmouth, The New Forest Sport and Recreation Study, The New Forest Committee, 1996.

22. Ecotec Research and Consulting Limited, Tourism in the New Forest 1991-92, report on the tourism survey to the New Forest District Council, Southern Tourist Board and New Forest Tourism, 1992.

23. Forestry Commission, Enjoying the Forest – Recreation 2000. An access and recreation plan for the Crown lands of the New Forest. Consultation draft. Forestry Commission, July 2000.

24. Ecotec Research and Consulting Limited, Tourism in the New Forest 1991-92, report on the tourism survey to the New Forest District Council, Southern Tourist Board and New Forest Tourism, 1992.

4 Identifying the draft National Park boundary

The boundary for the New Forest National Park must be based on the statutory criteria for National Parks set out in the 1949 Act. In drawing the detail of the draft boundary the Agency has also taken into account the approach it agreed in July 2000 (see Chapter 2).

The Agency's draft National Park boundary for the New Forest has been guided by the technical study carried out by consultants ERM – see Appendix C. This document draws extensively on their technical advice.

This consultation document explains in full the Agency's reasoning for the draft boundary, section by section, based on National Park criteria. The Agency is now asking for your views on the proposal – again, based on these criteria.

Factors considered

Administrative, physical and cultural factors were considered in order to define the area that needed to be looked at to identify a draft boundary. The area considered extended:

- in the east – to the edge of Southampton Water;
- in the south – to the Solent Coast, excluding built-up areas around Christchurch;
- in the west and north – to approximately 5 km beyond the existing Heritage Area boundary to include the Avon valley and up to the edge of the Wiltshire chalk downlands.

Administratively the New Forest lies mainly in New Forest District. The New Forest perambulation lies at the heart, enclosing the principal areas of forest and heath.

The starting point for identifying the boundary was land within the New Forest Heritage Area, the South Hampshire AONB, and the New Forest Countryside Character Area/Natural Area, jointly defined by the Countryside Agency and English Nature. However, several other important natural and cultural influences were also taken into account in defining the area which needed to be considered.

Topography, geology and land use

Geologically the New Forest occupies the centre of the Hampshire Basin – a downfold in the underlying chalk strata that was filled by sedimentation, raised above sea level as a flat plateau, then capped by peri-glacial gravels. A distinct topographic and geological unit, the outer, most fertile parts have been enclosed for farming and the less fertile central areas are forest and heath.

Commoning

The creation of a Royal Hunting Forest in 1079 formalised a situation whereby settled communities on the relatively fertile soils shared the heath and woodland resources at the heart of the area. The amount of land with common rights attached is a good indication of the extent of this system of land management in the New Forest. It has changed relatively little through time. The most recent map dates from 1989[25] and shows a 5 to 10 km-wide band of land with commoning rights attached, all around the edge of the New Forest perambulation.

Forest law and the perambulations

The New Forest perambulation defines the area covered by historic Forest law and rights of common. The 'Large Bounds' perambulation of 1227–1300 extended to the River Avon in the west, to the Hampshire county boundary in the north, and to the coast in the east and south. From 1327 until the New Forest Act of 1964, the much smaller 'Small Bounds' perambulation (similar in extent to the modern day one) was the definitive area for legal purposes. The current perambulation was defined in 1964.

Cultural perceptions

A less distinct set of boundaries for the New Forest can be found in well-known writings about its landscape, such as those of Gilpin[26] and Wise[27]. They were highly influential in the New Forest's rise to popularity for recreation. In general these writers perceived the New Forest as extending westwards to the River Avon, and east and south to the coast. The northern boundary was less distinct.

The appraisal process

The New Forest's natural beauty and recreational appeal depend on its distinctive combination of visual, nature conservation, historical and land management characteristics as well as intangible features (such as the feelings it evokes). Most, if not all, of these originate from the same traditional system of land use and management.

There is clear evidence that this system used to extend to the adjacent coastal and river valley landscapes. In developing the draft New Forest National Park boundary we have included these landscapes where they are of exceptional natural beauty and offer outstanding recreational opportunities.

All land within the National Park should meet the statutory criteria for designation. The aim in drawing up a draft New Forest National Park boundary is to:

- consider including all types of landscape that are linked to the Forest;

- include high quality habitats and sites of nature conservation interest, especially coastal grazing marshes and floodplain grasslands of national, European and international importance;

- take in important peripheral historic landscapes such as the river terrace landscapes of the Avon valley and their associated features;

- consider bringing into the National Park the core commoning areas, as well as areas capable of providing backup grazing, and areas formerly characterised by open grazing;

- include marginal areas that need to be managed in conjunction with the Forest core, especially those which offer opportunities for enjoying the area without damaging its special qualities.

25. Stagg, D and Page, J, Two Reports on New Forest Commoning (CCD 45), Countryside Commission, 1989.

26. Gilpin, W, Remarks on Forest Scenery, T Cadell and W Davies, 1791.

27. Wise, J R, The New Forest: Its History and Scenery, Smith Elder, 1863.

The following considerations were taken into account for each boundary section.

Statutory criteria
Natural beauty

- Landscape considerations: landscape character, landscape quality (condition, presence of key characteristics), visual and functional links with the Forest, intangible landscape qualities.

- Ecological considerations: habitat character and features, important semi-natural habitats, continuity with Forest habitats.

- Historical and cultural considerations: historic landscape character and features, historical and built environment designations, cultural links with the Forest and its traditional management system.

- Commoning considerations: recent use for backup grazing, potentially suited to backup grazing, local need for backup grazing, whether an area was once grazed in conjunction with the open forest.

Opportunities for open-air recreation

- Existing and potential opportunities for understanding and enjoying the area's special qualities, and for quiet open-air activities.

- Scope for integrated management with the Forest core to help conserve the quality of the recreational experience in the New Forest as a whole.

- Accessibility, particularly by sustainable means.

In general, greater emphasis has been put on the **quality** of the landscape and recreational experience, and less upon character than was used in defining the boundary for the New Forest Heritage Area.

Detailed boundary considerations

The draft boundary which was then drawn up was based on the criteria for National Parks and the following additional considerations.

- Where possible, the draft boundary uses roads and other features, such as rivers, as physical limits to the area. However, the limit of a particular type of landscape has sometimes also been used as a guide. In some areas this means that it has been necessary to use field boundaries to define the draft National Park boundary. Where the boundary is at the coast it has generally been drawn to follow the low water mark (LWM).

- Where the existing boundary for the New Forest Heritage Area or AONB works well it has been retained.

- Care has been taken to avoid subdividing marginal towns and villages. At Ringwood the Green Belt, as defined in the adopted local plan, generally offers a good boundary for the National Park.

- In some areas the boundaries of existing designations have been followed to include valuable features and also for clarity and convenience. In the Avon valley, for example, there are many areas on the edge of the boundary that are designated as being of national or international nature conservation or historical importance.

- The appraisal process also took account of the planning context by references to all the relevant structure plans, local plans and minerals and waste local plans. The aim was to ensure that the recommended boundary is consistent with planning policies: in particular, whether land is to be subject to quarrying or to major industrial or commercial development (that is, where this is shown in adopted development plans).

- Marginal land that is being used for sand and gravel extraction or as landfill sites has been included, provided it will be restored and after restoration will make a strong positive contribution to the area's landscapes, habitats or recreational opportunities.

Chapters 5 and 6 show how these considerations were applied in identifying a draft boundary.

Areas needing particular consideration

The following areas were given particular consideration:

- where the Heritage Area (or South Hampshire AONB) boundary generally meets the National Park criteria and has stood the test of time in planning terms, including:
  - much of the eastern boundary along the waterside;
  - the southern boundary between Lymington and Christchurch;
  - most of the northern boundary between Fordingbridge and the A3090.

- where major changes in the boundary should be considered, particularly:
  - land north of Totton, including part of the M27 corridor: bringing this land into the Heritage Area has been considered at several local plan inquiries;
  - Dibden Bay, where the Heritage Area does not meet the coast and where there are proposals for port development;
  - Calshot, where new boundaries would need to be drawn taking in land from both the Heritage Area and the AONB;
  - Lymington, where an important issue is whether or not to include the town within the National Park;
  - the Avon valley south of Ringwood, which contains outstanding water meadows;
  - the Avon valley between Ringwood and Fordingbridge, where the Heritage Area boundary has been considered at two local plan inquiries.

Although all areas of the boundary were examined closely, these six areas were looked at particularly thoroughly, with more detailed landscape field surveys and backup grazing research being undertaken. For each of these areas, a number of boundary options were developed and their relative merits explored and tested through desk and field survey.

5 An overview of the draft boundary

The draft boundary (see Map A and maps 1–20) is described here in four broad sectors – East, South, West and North – drawing on the New Forest District Landscape Character Assessment[28]. This describes the landscape, habitat and historical character of the broad landscape character areas, highlighting important environmental features.

Each broad sector is described in terms of the:

- general landscape context and relationship to the existing Heritage Area and/or AONB boundaries;

- key principles that have influenced the definition of the draft National Park boundary within the sector;

- draft boundary, including the main landscape, ecological, historical, grazing and recreational interests that have been included.

See also Chapter 6 for more detail of the 17 draft boundary sections and the reasons why each section has been included.

The East – Totton and the waterside
(boundary sections 1–9, maps 1–6)

Background
On the eastern edge of the New Forest there is a clear topographic edge. The ridge line above Southampton Water provides long views both to and from the Forest.

Before the Second World War the area was largely undeveloped enclosed farmland. This was strongly linked, both visually and through usage, to the Forest core and to the water's edge where there were extensive coastal grazing marshes and a series of historic tide mill settlements. Much of this original character was lost in the 1950s and 1960s when the waterside became an area of major residential and industrial development for Southampton. The link to the water's edge now survives in only three main areas: at Eling, Dibden Bay and Ashlett Creek, just north of Fawley Power Station. (There is also a fourth link at Frostlane between the eastern edge of Hythe and the Fawley Refinery Complex, but this is narrow and tenuous.) The New Forest Heritage Area boundary broadly follows the top of the ridge line and the A326, but extends to include these three areas.

At Dibden Bay extensive land reclamation took place in the 1960s and early 1970s using dredgings from container port development at Southampton. Here the Heritage Area boundary follows the former shoreline and does not include the reclaimed land. In the south at Calshot it excludes Calshot Point, although this land lies within the South Hampshire AONB.

Principles
The principles used for defining the draft boundary in this sector are to:

- maintain the principal strategic gaps where the Forest scenery

28. Environmental Resources Management, New Forest District Landscape Character Assessment, report to New Forest District Council, Hampshire County Council, The Countryside Agency and English Heritage, 2000.

meets the water's edge – these are an integral part of the New Forest landscape and have been very badly eroded;

- retain key views of the Forest from the outside – notably from the M27 westbound, from Mayflower Park and the city walls in Southampton, from the Southampton to Hythe ferry, and from boats and shipping on Southampton Water;

- include the coastal edge within the National Park where possible, in recognition of the fact that it is of European and international importance in nature conservation terms as a habitat for migratory birds, and of national importance in historic terms for its tide mill villages;

- recognise the important role of the waterside commons and coastal marshes in providing substantial areas of backup grazing with good access to the Forest core;

- encourage recreational access to the water's edge for walking, nature study and sailing by local residents, day visitors and holiday makers.

Draft boundary

The draft boundary is similar to that of the New Forest Heritage Area. The principal differences are extensions at Totton, Dibden, and Calshot. Because of the extensive urban development along the waterside, this is the most complex of the four boundary sectors.

North of Totton we propose that the boundary should extend as far

east as the River Blackwater, including Testwood Lakes. This is an integral part of the Forest landscape which, despite the intrusion of the M27, has a remarkably unspoilt ancient farmed character that is rich in Forest elements. The land is highly suited to backup grazing, for which there is a great need.

Including this area will help to maintain the landscape character and integrity of a 'gateway' that will provide most people's first impression of the National Park. There are rare long distance views from the ridge line at Hill Street across the Test valley. Part of the area falls within the Test Valley Environmentally Sensitive Area (ESA) and Testwood Lakes are used for quiet recreation.

Further south the draft boundary follows the A326 Totton Bypass, then includes the ancient forest farmlands, saltmarshes, intertidal mudflats and historic core of Eling village – all within the Heritage Area. After skirting Marchwood, again along the A326, the draft boundary includes the reclaimed foreshore at Dibden Bay. Although recently man-made, this is a remarkable, tranquil, wilderness landscape that fulfils a vital role as a setting for Southampton and enhances the approaches to the port by water. There are also impressive views eastwards from the higher ground above.

The coast is of European and international importance for nature conservation, having SPA and Ramsar designations.

Extensive areas of land are used for backup grazing in an area where there is considerable need.

Land at Dibden Bay is likely to be subject to an application for development of a major container port. However, the policies in the adopted development plans for the area do not allow for this unconditionally and development is not certain.

South of Dibden Bay the draft boundary is largely the same as that of the Heritage Area. It closely follows the edge of Hythe, Holbury, Langley, Blackfield and Fawley, enclosing a range of Forest core landscapes, heathland and semi-natural woodland.

At Ashlett, a historic village overlooking Southampton Water, the boundary again meets the coast. This gives the village a slightly larger coastal setting than the Heritage Area does. While the nature conservation importance of the adjoining salt marshes is recognised, in practical terms it would be difficult to include them in the National Park because they are physically isolated.

The boundary then follows the perimeter of Fawley Power Station. Although it is set in outstanding landscape, there are no grounds for including it in the National Park as decommissioning and restoration are not envisaged in the foreseeable future.

Beyond the power station the draft boundary includes Calshot Marshes, part of an SSSI that is of European and international importance. It has a wild, windswept character, outstanding views to Calshot Point, and quality grassland and marsh that would benefit from grazing. The point commands views across the mouth of Southampton Water. It is of outstanding importance for its geomorphology and for its castle, one of a series built by Henry VIII. There is also an outdoor activities centre.

The South – Solent Coast to Christchurch
(boundary sections 10–12, maps 7–12)

Background
The eastern part of this sector of the draft boundary, which runs along the Solent, is a sheltered, low-lying coastal landscape of country estates. Much of the land is intensively farmed but there are pockets with a heathy character. There are also areas of ancient woodland.

Marshy valleys with important wetland and brackish habitats drain southward to the Solent. Extensive areas of shingle and coastal marsh fringe the area, notably south of Calshot, at the mouths of the Beaulieu and Lymington Rivers, and inland of Hurst Point.

The central portion of this coastline, between Calshot and the Lymington River, lies within the New Forest Heritage Area. Much of it also lies within the New Forest perambulation. The South Hampshire AONB extends over a greater length of coastline, from Calshot Point to Hurst Point. Both the Heritage Area and AONB boundaries exclude the town of Lymington.

To the west of Hurst Point the coastal landscape around Christchurch Bay is dominated by built development at Milford on Sea, New Milton, Barton on Sea, Highcliffe and Christchurch. Here the Heritage Area boundary lies well inland of the coast, excluding not only the built-up areas but also much of the land between them where the landscape has been fragmented by development and has lost much of its traditional character.

Principles
The principles used for defining the draft boundary in this sector are to:
- maintain the integrity of the Solent Coast landscape, which is of acknowledged natural beauty, by extending the National Park designation to the whole coast between Calshot Point and Hurst Beach;
- include the ancient woodlands, coastal mudflats, saltmarshes and saline lagoons and coastal geomorphological features, all of which are of national and often European and international importance for nature conservation;
- include the town of Lymington because of its strong historical and cultural links with the Forest, the quality of its built environment, and its role as a centre for visitor services and sailing on the Solent;
- include sufficient land immediately west of Lymington along the valley of the Avon Water to provide a link between the Forest core and the coastal

marshes, which are potentially valuable for grazing and recreation;
- largely follow the Heritage Area boundary between Lymington and Christchurch where a more urban character prevails and where that boundary seems logical and generally accepted.

Draft boundary
The draft National Park boundary follows the low water mark from Calshot Point to Hurst Beach at Keyhaven. Like the AONB, it encompasses the Solent Coast and waterfront. Key characteristics of this stretch of coastline are its special sense of remoteness; its role as one of the largest surviving sections of undeveloped shore on England's south coast; and its outstanding views across the Solent to the Isle of Wight.

Its wooded coastal lowlands include lonely, intricate expanses of saltmarsh, tidal mudflats, shingle and the drowned estuaries of the Beaulieu and Lymington rivers which are of European and international importance for nature conservation.

Features of historical importance include Hurst Castle, part of the same series of coastal defences as Calshot Castle; the well preserved archaeological relics of medieval salt workings on the coast outside Lymington; and the charming coastal settlements of Bucklers Hard, Lymington and Keyhaven, which are all Conservation Areas.

Direct access to the coast is limited to Lepe Country Park, the

Solent Way, Lymington and Keyhaven but there is potential to improve public enjoyment. Much of the coastline is also of moderate value as backup grazing. Pennington and Keyhaven Marshes are grazed by cattle in summer. Pennington Common formerly linked them to the Forest.

The draft boundary includes Lymington because of the high quality of its townscape (the core is Georgian) and its strong visual links to surrounding countryside, particularly at Buckland, along the Lymington River, and in the area south of the town. Here the built-up area merges gradually with the gentle pastoral landscapes adjoining Pennington Marshes.

The town has very strong historical links with the Forest as, from around 1650, it was the principal port for Forest products. Today it is one of the foremost yachting centres of the Solent. The area attracts a lot of visitors and offers services such as accommodation. The inclusion of Lymington, which has good public transport links, within the National Park would enhance the scope for managing access and visitor pressure on the coast.

Between Hurst Beach and the A337 the draft boundary is similar to that of the AONB but includes the village of Keyhaven for its recreational importance. It follows the crest of a low ridge to the west of the Avon Water, enclosing areas of woodland and common at Upper Pennington.

West of Everton the draft boundary is the same as that of the Heritage Area. It excludes the urban fringe on the coastal plain between Lymington and Christchurch and includes ancient forest farmland and heath-associated estate landscapes. Most of the historical links between the Forest and this part of the coast have been lost.

The West – Avon valley
(boundary sections 13–15, maps 13–17)

Background

The Avon valley floodplain and river terraces meet the sea at the historic centre of Christchurch. They vary in width from around 4 km at Christchurch to less than 1 km in the north, near Downton. The Avon is best known as a chalk river valley, but south of Downton the chalk ends and the river water is supplemented by acid streams from the river terraces and New Forest heaths. This has helped to create a great variety of habitats.

Below Ringwood the river terrace landscapes, with their regular pattern of parliamentary enclosures, rise gently above the floodplain to meet the Forest edge landscapes, clearly visible because they are more wooded. Here the Heritage Area boundary has been tightly drawn to include the Forest edge landscapes and exclude the river terraces and floodplain landscapes.

On the west side of the valley, the river floodplain – with some very fine water meadow landscapes – is tightly enclosed by rising ground on which there are forestry plantations, heathland and

urban development. The Countryside Agency thinks that these landscapes beyond the river clearly belong to East Dorset, not the New Forest.

North of Ringwood the farmed landscapes of the river terraces have been extensively altered by gravel workings, restored as areas of water. However, the workings have had limited direct influence on the wider landscape because the original pattern of hedged drove roads has largely been retained, screening the gravel pits from view. North of Ibsley little extraction has occurred; the field patterns survive and there are increasingly strong visual links to the wooded escarpment that forms the edge of the New Forest perambulation.

The river meanders over a broad, flat floodplain. Above the floodplain there are open farmland and the conifer plantations of Ringwood Forest.

The Heritage Area boundary in this section of the valley has been contentious. The New Forest Committee and New Forest District Council wanted the boundary to extend westward to the A338 but the outcome of the 1997 New Forest District local plan inquiry was an intermediate boundary between the Gorley Road and the A338.

North of Fordingbridge, Forest edge landscapes meet the river floodplain and there is a strong tradition of using the meadows for backup grazing. Here the Heritage Area boundary was drawn to include much of the river floodplain to just south of Downton.

Principles

The principles used for defining the draft boundary in this sector are to:

- include high quality river terrace and floodplain landscapes, reflecting their function as an integral part of the traditional land management system and cultural heritage of the New Forest, plus their importance to views of the Forest;

- include not only the river itself but also the water meadows and wet gravel workings which are of European and international importance for their diverse wetland habitats, waders and wildfowl;

- conserve the many fine historic landscape features concentrated within and along the edge of the valley, including the river terrace parliamentary enclosure landscapes and drove roads, the remains of the water meadow systems, and the ancient settlements and river crossings;

- include valley bottom land – much of it an ESA – that is highly suitable for backup grazing for Forest stock;

- include areas with potential for quiet open air recreation, eg. extensive areas of tranquil wetland landscape that is suitable for walking, nature study and quiet recreational pursuits and that is within easy reach on foot of urban populations and seaside resorts.

Draft boundary

At the southern end of the Avon valley the draft National Park boundary follows the mainline railway and roads around the northern edge of Christchurch and its suburb, the modern village of Burton. It then turns northward along the western edge of the Avon floodplain, following the boundary of the Avon Valley ESA.

The coherence of the Avon valley and the Forest is very obvious when viewed from vantage points on the Dorset side such as St Catherine's Hill and Leybrook Common (not themselves within the draft National Park boundary). There are also similar, less dramatic views from the drove roads on the eastern side of the valley.

The draft boundary includes the tranquil water meadows in the valley bottom, which are of European and international importance for nature conservation, having SPA and Ramsar designations (the river itself is also a candidate SAC). The boundary also includes fine parliamentary enclosure landscapes and drove roads on the eastern terraces above the river, and the Conservation Area at Sopley. The land in the valley bottom is well suited to backup grazing.

The recreational potential of this section of the valley is very high: it is directly linked to the historic centre of Christchurch by the Avon Valley Path and there are also good footpath routes into the Forest

core.

Ringwood has been isolated from its landscape setting within the Forest by the A31 and no longer contributes to Forest character. The Agency therefore proposes that it should be excluded from the National Park, as it has been from the Heritage Area. The draft boundary follows the edge of the built-up area.

Moving north, the draft boundary again runs along the western edge of the Avon Valley ESA, including land of high nature conservation interest and a number of small historic settlements. The flood meadow landscapes of this section are less remarkable and less accessible than those further south, but Blashford Lakes are of high value for recreation and environmental interpretation. Mineral workings have been, or will be, restored to an appropriate use.

North of Fordingbridge, which the Agency thinks should be outside the proposed National Park area because of extensive modern development, the draft boundary is similar to that of the Heritage Area. However, it includes additional floodplain land.

It also includes the remarkable village of Breamore on the western edge of the floodplain opposite Woodgreen. This is a historic river crossing point with a rare manorial green. It is designated as an SSSI and a Conservation Area. Before the perambulation was fenced it was grazed in conjunction with the open forest (unenclosed Crown land over which grazing takes place).

The North – Wiltshire and Test valley
(boundary sections 16–17, maps 18–20)

Background

The northern edge of the New Forest lies mainly on London clay within the upper catchment of the River Blackwater. Here the ancient forest farmland landscape – with extensive areas of deciduous woods and wood pasture – stretches up towards the Wiltshire chalk downs.

Just below the edge of the chalk there is a subtle change in character as the mainly open arable landscape of the downs meets the more wooded landscape of the New Forest. At this point there are long views southwards across the Forest.

Further east the River Blackwater separates the New Forest from Romsey Common. Although the landscapes of Romsey Common are similar in many respects to those south of the Blackwater, they are not part of the traditional New Forest pastoral system as they have no Forest grazing rights attached, only rights to graze adjacent commons[29].

Principles

The principles used for defining the draft boundary in this sector are to:

- exclude the chalkland landscapes and settlements plus areas that are not part of the traditional New Forest pastoral system;
- include sites of national importance for nature conservation, such as the many ancient deciduous woodlands, remnant wood pasture and heathland commons;
- include, where possible, historic landscape features, particularly areas of medieval assarts, deer parks, sunken drove roads and lanes;
- include satellite commons that could be brought back into use for grazing in conjunction with the open forest or that could absorb additional recreational use.

Draft boundary

The draft National Park boundary for these sections is the same as the existing Heritage Area boundary. In the west it follows a small ridge line and valley up from the Avon valley to North Charford where there are fine views over Forest landscapes to the east.

The attractive settlement of Downton is excluded because its character and setting clearly indicate its association with the underlying chalk. The mainly modern settlements of Woodfalls and Morgan's Vale are also excluded, but Redlynch – which has the distinctive linear settlement pattern of this part of the Forest – is included.

Eastwards the draft boundary follows lanes, field boundaries and the woodland edge as far as Plaitford Green, enclosing a number of important and extensive SSSIs, notably Loosehanger Copse, Langley Wood and the remnant wood pasture of Whiteparish Common. Beyond Plaitford Green, within a more open landscape, the boundary includes pastoral streamside landscapes and a number of distinctive Forest settlements.

29. Stagg, D and Page, J, Two Reports on New Forest Commoning (CCD 45), Countryside Commission, 1989.

6 The draft boundary in detail

Table 3 gives full details of the draft boundary for a New Forest National Park, section by section, and the reasons why the Countryside Agency has included each area. These are based on the statutory criteria of natural beauty and opportunities for recreation and take into account the Agency's approach to defining a National Park boundary. The table should be read in conjunction with the maps at the back of this document.

- Column 1 describes the draft boundary line.

- Column 2 summarises the natural beauty of land within the boundary, examining landscape, nature conservation, historical and commoning considerations. The terms used in the table to characterise landscape (eg. enclosed valley sides, heath associated smallholdings and dwellings) are drawn from the New Forest District Landscape Character Assessment[30].

- Column 3 reviews the recreational opportunities within the draft boundary.

- Column 4 covers detailed boundary considerations including any options that have been considered, and the reasons why particular areas have been included or excluded in the initial proposed boundary.

30. Environmental Resources Management, New Forest District Landscape Character Assessment, report to New Forest District Council, Hampshire County Council, The Countryside Agency and English Heritage, 2000.

Table 3.
The draft boundary and the reasoning behind it (the landscape types are described in Appendix D)

Boundary section	Natural beauty	Recreation	Detailed boundary considerations
1. North of Totton (Map 1) Draft boundary runs from A3090/A36 junction along River Blackwater and New Forest District Council boundary, including Testwood Lakes. It then follows the northern built-up edge of Totton.	**Landscape** • Landscape types: enclosed valley sides; heath associated smallholdings and dwellings – strong Forest character • Remarkably unspoilt, rich in Forest elements • First view of the New Forest for many visitors • Fine long-distance views over the Test valley **Ecology** • Mixture of arable and grassland • Includes part of Test Valley ESA, east of Hill Street **History** • Bounds of the Forest extended to the Blackwater until 1300 • Parliamentary and small parliamentary enclosures, well preserved and complete, also valley floor • Drove roads, eg. Wade Hill Drove **Commoning** • Several areas of backup grazing • Wade Hill Drove still occasionally drift grazed • Highly suitable for backup grazing, high level of need from nearby commoners • May be scope for backup grazing within the ESA and, in future, around Testwood Lakes	• Potential Forest gateway • Good network of rights of way • Testwood Lokes to be used for informal recreation and nature study • Good access from adjoining areas of Totton	• Testwood Lakes are an area of gravel extraction (restoration to water and recreation by 2003) • Draft boundary not extended to include Teswood Marshes SSSI because of its physical isoltation from the rest of the National Park and the dominance of Totton

Boundary section	Natural beauty	Recreation	Detailed boundary considerations
2. Totton Bypass (Map 1) Draft boundary follows western edge of bypass from Loperwood to Colbury Farm.	**Landscape** • Landscape types: ancient forest farmlands; heath associated smallholdings and dwellings • Landscape in good condition; clear and visually–obvious edge to the Forest **Ecology** • Mainly arable; no relevant designations **History** • Assarts, small parliamentary fields, drove roads **Commoning** • Several commoners' holdings and some backup grazing	• Important peripheral area to Forest • Some rights of way and potential for local access	
3. Eling (Map 2) Draft boundary follows southern edge of Totton, includes historic village of Eling and land to low water mark as far east as Bury Marsh, then returns to the A326, excluding industrial and gravel working areas.	**Landscape** • Landscape types: ancient forest farmlands; coastal fringe • Well-wooded landscape with traditional field patterns, good condition • Strong visual links between the Forest and the tranquil water's edge **Ecology** • Arable rotation, semi-natural woodland, quality grassland and marsh • Eling and Bury Marshes SSSI - saltmarshes and intertidal mudflats of European and international importance, having SPA, Ramsar and candidate SAC designations **History** • Well-preserved assarts and small wavy fields • Eling is a Conservation Area with historic bridge and tide mill; important medieval/post-medieval transport node • Drove roads - Trotts Lane and Jacob's Gutter Lane **Commoning** • Marshes were formerly commons; forest grazing rights throughout the area; vicinage practised until 1960s • Several areas of backup grazing • Highly suitable for backup grazing; high level of need from nearby commoners	• Eling is an important tourist attraction • Open space and access to the water's edge; well used for walking and picnicking • Good rights of way network, existing and proposed	• Area of larger, arable fields and gravel extraction south of Bury Farm (restoration to agriculture, 2008) is excluded because landscape is in poor condition
4. Marchwood (Map 2) Draft boundary follows western edge of A326 around Marchwood.	**Landscape** • Landscape types: ancient forest farmlands; heath associated smallholdings and dwellings • Strongly wooded character clearly marking edge of Forest **Ecology** • Mixture of arable and semi-natural woodlands **History** • Small parliamentary fields and assarted woodland, some medieval • Drove roads **Commoning** • Several areas of backup grazing	• Potential to improve access to this area from Marchwood	

Boundary section	Natural beauty	Recreation	Detailed boundary considerations
5. Dibden Bay (Map 3) Draft boundary follows south-east edge of Marchwood and edge of military port. Includes all the reclaimed land and foreshore to low water mark. On the south side, draft boundary follows the edge of the built-up area of Hythe.	**Landscape** • Landscape types: ancient forest farmlands; coastal fringe • Strong character and good condition; contrast between the two landscape types • Largest surviving visual and functional link from edge of Forest to the waterside • Long views over Southampton Water, and towards the Forest from Southampton city centre, the Hythe ferry and other shipping • Sense of tranquillity within the farmland area, and wilderness along the coastal fringe **Ecology** • Quality grassland and marsh, arable land and some woodland • Foreshore area is part of Hythe to Calshot Marshes SSSI – saltmarsh and mudflats of European and international importance, having SPA and Ramsar designations • Inland area is Site of Importance for Nature Conservation (SINC), indicating that it is of critical importance for nature conservation within the New Forest District. **History** • Historic landscape types: coastal, small, wavy fields, assarts inland **Commoning** • Majority of the reclaimed land is in use as backup grazing; also numerous areas around Dibden village • Reclaimed land is largest single area of semi-natural grassland in the vicinity of the New Forest perambulation • Highly suitable for backup grazing; high level of need with many commoners nearby	• Outstanding oasis of tranquil, wild character • Crossed by an important public right of way linking Hythe to Marchwood • Potential to expand rights of way network • Next to Hythe Marina	• Application for a port development is expected: development plans do not, however, make provision for this unconditionally • Whole area is subject to Strategic Gap policy in adopted structure plan and local plan
6. Hythe to Langley (Maps 4 and 5) Draft boundary follows western edge of A326 Hythe Bypass, includes land inside the bypass at Denny Lodge, then closely follows the edge of the built-up area around Holbury and Langley. Most of the land is within the New Forest perambulation, which generally abuts the built-up area.	**Landscape** • Landscape types: timber inclosures and plantations; heath associated smallholdings and dwellings; coastal plain estates (large informal enclosures); heath associated estates • High quality woodland and heathland landscape, rich in ancient features **Ecology** • Woodland, heathland, some arable • Dibden and Fawley inclosures, next to Hythe, and areas at Langley are part of New Forest SSSI • SSSI of European and international importance, having SPA, Ramsar and candidate SAC designations **History** • Historic landscape types are heathland plantation, heathland, parliamentary fields • Numerous Bronze Age burial barrows • Holbury Manor Scheduled Ancient Monument **Commoning** • Active commoning area and backup grazing on enclosed land at Roughdown • Open forest grazing within the perambulation	• Outstanding – mainly open access land • Adjacent to settlements – intensive local use • Parking at Dibden Inclosure and Blackwell Common	• Draft boundary includes Holbury Landfill (programmed for restoration to grassland in 1997, but extension of time for tipping granted in 1999)

Boundary section	Natural beauty	Recreation	Detailed boundary considerations
7. Langley to Fawley (Map 6) Draft boundary follows edge of built-up areas of Langley, Blackfield and Fawley, then B3053, enclosing land that is outside the perambulation.	**Landscape** • Landscape types: coastal plain estates (large informal enclosures) around Stanswood valley, a fine wooded valley landscape with heath and common above **Ecology** • Mainly arable and scrub, but woodland within the valley • North Solent SSSI, with important wetland habitats, extends all along the Stanswood valley and borders on the built-up area at Blackfield **History** • Historic landscape types are parks, common (Badminston Common) and parliamentary fields **Commoning** • Small areas of backup grazing • Gravel extraction areas offer potential for backup grazing after restoration	• An extensive rights of way network connects settlements, valley and coast	• There are gravel workings at Fields Farm (restoration to agriculture, date to be agreed)
8. Ashlett Creek (Map 6) Draft boundary encloses the small valley of Ashlett Creek, mainly following field boundaries.	**Landscape** • Landscape types: coastal plain estates (large informal enclosures); coastal fringe • High quality landscapes contained within a small valley, with dramatic view across salt marshes and Southampton Water • Tranquil, peaceful character **Ecology** • Grassland, arable, scrub, saltmarsh • Part of Hythe to Calshot Marshes SSSI, which is of European and international importance, having SPA, Ramsar and candidate SAC designations **History** • Coastal historic landscape type • Attractive coastal village and Conservation Area **Commoning** • A high proportion of land within the valley is believed to be in use as backup grazing, and the coastal marshes have been grazed within the last 15 years • Vicinage practised until 1960s • Land highly suitable for backup grazing; high level of need with many commoners nearby	• Important centre for sailing, with public access • Public footpath to Calshot • Popular with visitors as one of the few surviving areas of traditional waterside character	• Extension of the National Park boundary to include saltmarsh within the SSSI would be difficult in practical terms as it would be an isolated parcel between Fawley Refinery and power station

Boundary section	Natural beauty	Recreation	Detailed boundary considerations
9. Calshot (Map 6) Draft boundary follows perimeter of power station site, then south side of inlet to sea, then low water mark to Calshot Point.	**Landscape** • Landscape types: coastal plain estates (large informal enclosures); coastal fringe • Point commands view of Southampton Water and the Solent (but also the power station) • Wide open space, dramatic windswept character **Ecology** • Quality grassland and marsh • Part of the Hythe to Calshot Marshes SSSI, which is of European and international importance, having SPA, Ramsar and candidate SAC designations; Calshot Marshes are a Local Nature Reserve owned by Hampshire County Council • Calshot Spit is of geomorphological importance and is part of the North Solent SSSI **History** • Coastal historic landscape • Calshot Castle is a Scheduled Ancient Monument managed by English Heritage and is one of a series of coastal defences built by Henry VIII • Historic association with the flying boats **Commoning** • Backup grazing around Ower and Calshot village • Historically strong links between marshes and Forest, with vicinage • Area in general is highly suitable for backup grazing; high level of need with many commoners nearby • Opportunities after mineral extraction to restore land to backup grazing	• At Calshot Point there is a major centre for outdoor pursuits, run by Hampshire County Council; activities include sailing, angling, windsurfing, canoeing and other watersports • Calshot Marshes offer opportunities for nature study, birdwatching and quiet enjoyment	• Draft boundary includes all of the South Hampshire AONB • Includes gravel extraction at Badminston Farm (restoration to agriculture c2013). The option of excluding this land was considered but rejected as restoration may provide land for backup grazing
10. Solent Coast (Maps 7 to 9) Draft boundary follows low water mark from Calshot Point to Lymington River. The coastline between the Beaulieu River and Pylewell lies within the New Forest perambulation.	**Landscape** • Landscape types: coastal fringe; coastal plain estates (large informal enclosures and, close to Lymington, small parliamentary enclosures) • Sheltered, low-lying landscape with a strong sense of place – area where the Forest meets the sea, views to and from the Isle of Wight • Together with land from Lymington to Hurst Point, forms one of the largest surviving sections of undeveloped coastline on England's south-east coast – a single coherent physiographic unit **Ecology** • Ancient semi-natural coastal woodland, arable and grassland • Coastal mudflats, marshes and reedbed • North Solent SSSI, which is of European and international importance, having SPA, Ramsar and candidate SAC designations **History** • Mix of historic landscape types: coastal, parks, parliamentary fields, small parliamentary fields, small wavy fields • Cadland House and Pylewell Park are on the English Heritage Historic Parks and Gardens Register **Commoning** • Open forest grazing extends to the water's edge, eg. near the mouth of the Beaulieu River • Very active commoning area	• Area with great scope for quiet enjoyment, solitude, birdwatching • Includes Lepe Country Park • Otherwise limited public access, except via the Solent Way and the foreshore itself	• This whole stretch of coastline lies within the South Hampshire AONB

Boundary section	Natural beauty	Recreation	Detailed boundary considerations
11. Lymington River to Everton **(Maps 9 and 10)** Draft boundary follows low water mark from Lymington River past Hurst Point and Hurst Beach before turning inland. Includes Keyhaven village, then follows AONB boundary along a low ridge above the Avon Water to A337.	**Landscape** • Landscape types: coastal fringe; coastal plain estates (small parliamentary enclosures) • Very quiet, remote stretch of coastline with a strong pastoral character and many ancient features • Stunning views to Isle of Wight from Keyhaven and Hurst Point **Ecology** • Extensive areas of quality grassland and marsh • Hurst Castle and Lymington River Estuary SSSI, which is of European and international importance, having SPA, Ramsar and candidate SAC designations; Lymington to Keyhaven Coastal Nature Reserve • Marshes were formerly salterns converted to grazing land with the decline of the salt industry in the 19th century • Geomorphological and biological importance – unique shingle ridges and spit **History** • Historic landscape types: coastal, small parliamentary and small wavy fields – patterns complete and well-preserved • Conservation Areas at Buckland (north of Lymington), Lymington and Keyhaven. The District Council is in the process of designating a further Conservation Area at Lymington (Waterford) • Scheduled Ancient Monuments include an Iron Age hillfort at Buckland (one of a series that ringed the Forest) and Hurst Castle, part of Henry VIII's coastal defences • Lymington has a historic core (medieval, but mainly Georgian) fronting the river, plus extensive 19th and 20th-century development. It is a charming coastal town, with pleasing brick and render architecture. It has a strong visual relationship to the river • The town has cultural and historical importance as the principal port of trade for Forest products from around 1650, and a centre for the salt trade and piracy **Commoning** • Keyhaven and Lymington Marshes grazed by cattle in summer • Historically, closely linked to the open forest, other commons and the coastal grazing marshes by a series of drove roads – vicinage was practised • Land is of moderate to high suitability for backup grazing. Suitability is constrained by cost: land is too expensive for commoners' ponies • Local need for grazing is not as high as in some other areas	• Lymington is a busy tourist destination and one of the principal centres of visitor accommodation in the Forest • Lymington (and to a lesser extent Keyhaven) is a major sailing centre for the Solent, with marinas and sailing clubs • Ferries from Lymington to the Isle of Wight and from Keyhaven to Hurst Point in summer • Other sections of the coastline are very quiet and accessible only via the Solent Way – potential for quiet enjoyment, solitude, birdwatching • Particular need for management of access to this section of the coast	• Lymington included because of its high quality townscape, strong relationship with landscape setting, visitor accommodation, and need for integrated visitor management • Manor Farm, Pennington, an extensive sand, gravel and landfill site (restoration to agriculture, 2007), included because it may provide backup grazing

Boundary section	Natural beauty	Recreation	Detailed boundary considerations
12. Everton to Highcliffe (Maps 11 and 12) Draft boundary skirts built-up areas of Everton, Hordle, New Milton and Highcliffe, then joins mainline railway	**Landscape** • Landscape types: draft boundary guided by southern edge of ancient forest farmlands, heath associated smallholdings and dwellings and heath associated estates • These landscapes are in good condition and have a strong Forest character, whereas the coastal plain estates landscape to the south has many incongruous features **Ecology** • Mixture of woodland and arable with some areas of grassland • Pennington Common and Upper Pennington Common are part of the New Forest SSSI **History** • Small parliamentary enclosures and small wavy fields in east, parks (such as Hinton Park) and plantations further west • Drove roads and connections to the coast largely lost **Commoning** • Several active commoning areas within the boundary, for instance near Mount Pleasant and Bashley • Moderate to high level of need for backup grazing	• Area lies close to the Forest core and is linked to it by a number of rights of way • Potential to develop footpath network to provide access to the open forest from urban areas to the south	• Option of including additional land at Walkford Brook was considered and rejected (landscape condition mixed, no significant potential for backup grazing, limited access)
13. Avon valley below Ringwood (Maps 13 to 15) Draft boundary follows mainline railway to B3347, then north around Burton on minor roads, then briefly joins A35. At the Avon Valley Path it turns and runs northwards following field boundaries along the edge of the floodplain. **The boundary excluding Ringwood is included in this section.**	**Landscape** • Landscape types: river floodplain; river terrace farmlands • High quality tranquil flood meadows and fine enclosed landscapes • Outstanding views across the Avon valley to the Forest from high ground on the edge of the Dorset Heaths, eg. at St Catherine's Hill and Leybrook Common • Complementary, although less dramatic views, outward from the Forest, from drove roads descending into the Avon valley **Ecology** • Arable and grassland (especially in floodplain north of Burton), small woodlands • Avon Valley SSSI with hay meadows, pastures, fens, mires and riparian woods, plus internationally important wildfowl and wader habitat; associated acid grassland on eastern river terraces is of European and international importance, having SPA and Ramsar designations • River Avon SSSI, which is a candidate SAC, and Avon Valley ESA **History** • Small wavy and small parliamentary fields, valley floor – well preserved • Numerous drove roads that formerly provided strong links from Forest to valley floor • Conservation Area at Sopley **Commoning** • Several areas of common and water meadow, plus land near Sopley and Ripley currently used as backup grazing • ESA land highly suitable for backup grazing, moderate to high level of grazing need	• Directly accessible from historic centre of Christchurch via Avon Valley Path • Good rights of way network on river terrace farmlands, especially in south • Boundary includes all the Avon Valley Path to Ringwood • Limited existing opportunities for enjoyment of tranquil water meadows –- but future potential	• The draft boundary brings in land from Dorset (Christchurch Borough and East Dorset District) at southern end of the valley • Generally follows the western edge of the ESA in order to include all valuable meadowland • Excludes the built-up area of Ringwood. Town formerly provided a livestock market for the Forest, and has a historic centre. However, the townscape is now dominated by the A31T and by extensive modern development

Boundary section	Natural beauty	Recreation	Detailed boundary considerations
14. Avon valley: Ringwood to Fordingbridge (Maps 15 and 16) Draft boundary follows western edge of Avon floodplain.	**Landscape** • Landscape types: river floodplain; river terrace farmlands; gravel/mineral extraction • Strong wetland character: extensive areas of tranquil meadowland, wet gravel workings restored to water, and enclosed farmland next to the Forest perambulation • Open forest visible above • Wet gravel workings fit well within the landscape – limited visibility; old drove roads and hedgerows have been retained **Ecology** • Arable plus extensive grassland in valley floor • Avon Valley SSSI (see boundary section 13, Avon valley below Ringwood) includes former gravel workings at Blashford Lakes, which are of European and international importance, having SPA and Ramsar designations • River Avon SSSI, which is a candidate SAC, and Avon Valley ESA **History** • Historic landscape types: valley floor and small parliamentary fields – complete and well-preserved north of Ibsley • Considerable evidence of Bronze and Iron Age activity • Conservation Areas at Ibsley and Bickton, medieval bridge at Fordingbridge, many drove roads **Commoning** • There are several practising commoners within the area: some use quite large areas of water meadows for summer grazing • Historically very strong links with the Forest; very active commoning area before the perambulation was fenced in the 1960s, leading to loss of open grazing • Competition for grazing from recreational horse-keeping • Valley land highly suitable for backup grazing and high level of need, with many commoners nearby along the Forest edge	• A very tranquil landscape away from the main road, the A338, • Most of the Avon Valley Path falls within the draft National Park boundary • Blashford Lakes have an interpretive centre and are used for birdwatching, fishing and some active watersports	• Draft boundary generally follows western edge of the ESA, including fine water meadow landscapes • Blashford Lakes and several active gravel workings are included – for ecological and recreational reasons • Active gravel workings are Snails Lane, Ellingham (restoration to water storage and recreation, 2001), Ringwood Pit, Ellingham (water storage and recreation, 2002) and Mockbeggar (restoration to agriculture, 2003) • No additional gravel extraction is expected to be permitted in future – no preferred areas identified in adopted minerals local plan

Boundary section	Natural beauty	Recreation	Detailed boundary considerations
15. Avon valley north of Fordingbridge (Map 17) Draft boundary follows edge of floodplain, then A338, includes village of Breamore, rejoins A338, then crosses to east side of floodplain at Searchfield Farm.	**Landscape** • Landscape types: river floodplain plus a small section of river terrace farmlands to the west • High quality pastoral character, strong sense of history • Very strong visual and functional links to Forest – scarp and perambulation adjoin and overlook the floodplain at Castle Hill, a famous Forest viewpoint **Ecology** • Quality grassland and some arable • River Avon SSSI, Avon Valley ESA, and Breamore Marsh SSSI – an important surviving manorial green with goose and cattle grazing **History** • Valley floor, common and (at Breamore) old settlement historic landscape types • Woodgreen and Breamore form a Conservation Area • Historic river crossing between Woodgreen and Breamore • Considerable evidence of Roman and medieval activity **Commoning** • Breamore Marsh ran with the Forest until the 1960s • East of the river areas are grazed by Forest ponies and cattle, but there is little use of the valley floor	• Considerable potential, but access currently limited to a few points • Next to Forest parking at Castle Hill	• Draft boundary drawn fairly tightly around Breamore, excluding Breamore House and Park (although these are of considerable historical interest, they lie on the chalk) • Does not extend further north, as the influence of the underlying chalk becomes increasingly evident beyond Woodgreen
16. Searchfield Farm to Plaitford Green (Maps 18 and 19) Draft boundary follows small valley and ridge line to crest of scarp at North Charford, then eastwards across country along minor roads and field boundaries.	**Landscape** • Landscape types: heath associated smallholdings and dwellings, and ancient forest farmlands • Strong Forest edge landscape character, long views southward across the Forest from the north side of the Blackwater catchment, below the edge of chalk **Ecology** • Mixture of woodland and arable, with some grassland • Loosehanger Close, Langley Wood and Whiteparish Common SSSIs, including part of New Forest candidate SAC **History** • Assarts, commons, large wavy fields, plantations and drove roads • Many ancient features **Commoning** • Many 'satellite' commons, such as Whiteparish Common, lie outside the perambulation but could be revitalised by reintroducing grazing links to the open forest	• Quiet peripheral area outside the New Forest perambulation • May have scope to help relieve recreational pressures on Forest core • Good rights of way network	• Much of this section lies in Wiltshire (Salisbury District) • Excludes settlements of Woodfalls and Morgan's Vale; includes North Charford and Redlynch which have the distinctive linear settlement pattern of this part of the Forest

Boundary section	Natural beauty	Recreation	Detailed boundary considerations
17. Plaitford Green to A3090 (**Map 20**) Draft boundary follows ridge above the River Blackwater as far as Wellow Mill, then runs along the river itself as far as the A3090.	**Landscape** • Landscape type: small scale enclosed valley — the riverside landscape of the Blackwater valley • A more open landscape than Section 16, but one that still has a strong, coherent Forest edge character • Character merges gradually with the landscape of Romsey Common to the north-east **Ecology** • Arable (particularly north of the river) and woodland **History** • Intimate mix of historic landscape types: assarts, small wavy fields, valley floor, small parliamentary fields and plantations • Some Bronze Age sites • Traditional Forest settlements at West Wellow and Ham Down **Commoning** • Moderate suitability for backup grazing; high levels of need • Land within the boundary has rights to Forest grazing attached, while that to the north-east at Romsey Common does not	• Fair to good rights of way network • Proximity to motorway and trunk roads suggests the area may have a gateway role for visitors • Leisure park at Paulton's Park	• Land towards Romsey is excluded on topographic grounds and because it is not part of the traditional New Forest pastoral system

Appendix A

National Park legislation

National Parks are the most beautiful expanses of country in England and Wales where people can enjoy a wide range of open air recreation. The term National Park is a statutory title which recognises an area's national importance and provides the highest degree of protection for its landscape.

National Parks are part of a worldwide network of protected areas. In international terms they are classed as Category V protected landscapes by the World Conservation Union (IUCN). The objectives of Category V landscapes are "to maintain significant areas which are characteristic of the harmonious interaction of nature and culture, while providing opportunities for public enjoyment through recreation and tourism, and supporting the normal lifestyle and economic activity of these areas. These areas also serve scientific and educational purposes, as well as maintaining biological and cultural diversity."

Proposals for National Parks in England and Wales were first made in 1945 when the Government published a White Paper[31], written by John Dower. He gave shape to the concept of National Parks which remains valid today. He defined a National Park as:

"an extensive area of beautiful and relatively wild country in which, for the nation's benefit and by appropriate national decision and action:

- the characteristic landscape beauty is strictly preserved;
- access and facilities for open-air enjoyment are amply provided;
- wildlife and buildings and places of architectural and historic interest are suitably protected;
- while established farming use is effectively maintained."

Dower's recommendations were followed in 1947 by the Report of the National Parks Committee (commonly known as the Hobhouse Report, after its chairman, Sir Arthur Hobhouse)[32]. It recommended which areas should be selected as National Parks and proposed an administrative system for them.

Legislation, purposes and criteria

National Parks are designated under the National Parks and Access to the Countryside Act 1949. This Act implemented the findings of the Hobhouse Report, making provision for National Parks and establishing a National Parks Commission.

The 1949 Act was amended by the Countryside Act 1968 and the Environment Act 1995. Table 4 gives the National Park purposes and criteria from Section 5 of the Act and the definition of natural beauty from Section 114 as amended by the 1968 and 1995 Acts. This is the statutory basis for designating National Parks. It was

31. Dower, J, National Parks in England and Wales, HMSO, 1945

32. The National Parks Committee, Report of the National Parks Committee (England and Wales), HMSO, 1947

Table 4.

Extracts from the 1949 Act as amended by the 1968 and 1995 Acts

Statutory National Park purposes and criteria (Section 5)

(1) The provisions of this Part of this Act shall have effect for the purpose -

    (a) of conserving and enhancing the natural beauty, wildlife and cultural heritage of the areas specified in the next and following subsection; and

    (b) of promoting opportunities for the understanding and enjoyment of the special qualities of those areas by the public.

(2) The said areas are those extensive tracts of country in England and Wales as to which it appears to the Commission that by reason of –

    (a) their natural beauty, and

    (b) the opportunities they afford for open-air recreation, having regard both to their character and to their position in relation to centres of population,

it is especially desirable that the necessary measures shall be taken for the purposes mentioned in the last foregoing subsection.

The said areas, as for the time being designated by order made by the Commission and submitted to and confirmed by the Minister, shall be known as, and are hereinafter referred to as, National Parks.

Definition of natural beauty (Section 114)

References in this Act to the preservation, or conservation of the natural beauty of an area shall be construed as including references to the preservation or, as the case may be, the conservation, of its flora, fauna and geological and physiographical features.

reviewed by Sandford in 1974[33] and Edwards[34] in 1991 but it was decided that no major changes were required.

In 2000, in response to a request from the Government, The Countryside Agency reviewed the application of the criteria and decided that the key questions to be considered in designating new National Parks (other than natural beauty) were[35]:

Is it an extensive tract of country providing or capable of providing sufficient opportunities for open air recreation?

"We consider that the area needs to have characteristics that mark it out as different from the bulk of 'normal countryside'; so it needs more than simply a network of rights of way. It should contain qualities that might merit

investment to deliver a markedly superior recreational experience. While the countryside did not need to be rugged and open, a sense of relative wildness would be important."

Is it especially desirable to provide for the leadership of a national park authority, with the powers and duties laid down in the Environment Act 1995?"

"We consider that the designation must lead to the integrated management of the area and in particular in markedly better recreational experience than can be achieved by local authorities alone. This recreational experience must be available, promoted and interpreted to the 'socially excluded' as well as to the more mobile in the society, as a result of the work of the special authority."

33. Department of the Environment and Welsh Office, Report of the National Park Policies Review Committee, chaired by Lord Sandford, HMSO, 1974.

34. Edwards, R, Fit for the Future: Report of the National Parks Review Panel, Executive Summary (CCP 335), Countryside Commission, 1991.

35. Letter from Ewen Cameron, Chairman of the Countryside Agency, to the Rt Hon Michael Meacher, Minister for the Environment, 16 March 2000.

Appendix B

Designation history of the New Forest and the South Hampshire Coast AONB

1947

The New Forest, including its frontage to the Solent, was first proposed for designation[36] The first part of this section draws upon R Woolmore, Designation History Series: South Hampshire Coast AONB with New Forest Conservation Area, unpublished Countryside Agency paper, 1999 in the Report of the National Parks Committee[37] (the Hobhouse Report). This recommended that it should be considered as a Conservation Area (subsequently entitled Area of Outstanding Natural Beauty). The New Forest was not recommended as a National Park because of the management already afforded by the New Forest Verderers and the Forestry Commission.

1964

The National Parks Commission decided to review all proposals for coastal AONBs, including that part of the New Forest fronting the Solent.

1967

The South Hampshire Coast AONB was designated, an area extending from Calshot Point to Hurst Castle spit and including the Beaulieu estuary. This area, mainly outside the New Forest perambulation, is described[38] as "an area with a special sense of remoteness. Its wooded coastal lowlands include lonely intricate expanses of saltmarsh, tidal mudflats and shingle, and in places, embankments holding back brackish freshwater lagoons and marshes".

Early 1980s

The New Forest District Council developed the idea of a New Forest Heritage Area, recognising that the valued landscapes of the New Forest were not confined to the perambulation and that the core area was strongly influenced by the planning and management of the land outside it.

1986

The Forestry Commission established the New Forest Review Group (of which the Countryside Commission was a member) to examine measures to safeguard the New Forest and maintain its unique character.

The Review Group enthusiastically adopted the idea of the New Forest Heritage Area and recommended that it should be recognised at Government level as requiring special protection equivalent to a National Park. The Government agreed with this principle, recommended the establishment of a Heritage Area Committee (now called the New Forest Committee) and urged it to agree boundaries for the Heritage

36. The first part of this section draws upon R Woolmore, Designation History Series: South Hampshire Coast AONB with New Forest Conservation Area, unpublished Countryside Agency paper, 1999.

37. The National Parks Committee, Report of the National Parks Committee (England and Wales), HMSO, 1947.

38. Countryside Commission, Directory of Areas of Outstanding Natural Beauty (CCD 54), Countryside Commission, 1989.

Table 5.
New Forest Heritage Area boundary criteria

- To incorporate the land of outstanding national importance for its natural beauty, including flora, fauna, geological and physiographical features, and elements arising from human influences on the landscape, including archaeological, historical, cultural, architectural and vernacular features.

- To incorporate essential grazing land. This will include peripheral farmland which is or has recently been used as grazing land in conjunction with the New Forest, or which is part of an area which would be suitable to be utilised for grazing related to the Forest (whether with Forest Rights or not) so as in aggregate to include a sufficient pool of land to provide an adequate supply of back-up grazing land and the continued functioning of the historic dispersed pastoral regime relating to New Forest commoning in the long term. Convenience of access to the 'open forest' should also be considered in this context.

39. Land Use Consultants, New Forest Heritage Area: Proposed Boundary, report to the New Forest Committee, 1991.

40. Department of the Environment, PPG 7 (Revised): The Countryside: Environmental Quality and Economic and Social Development, HMSO, 1997.

41. Countryside Commission, Advice to Government on Protected Areas (CCP 532), Countryside Commission, 1998.

Area, incorporating essential grazing land as well as the best of the landscape around the Forest's perambulation.

1990

The New Forest Committee was established. This is an independent, non-statutory committee, co-ordinating the work of key Forest organisations which have responsibilities for the care of the Forest.

1991

The New Forest Committee commissioned Land Use Consultants (LUC) to define and describe in detail a boundary for the New Forest Heritage Area. LUC put forward boundary proposals in June[39], based on the two principal criteria shown in Table 5.

1994

The Government announced that the same planning policies would apply to the New Forest as to a National Park. This commitment was largely realised in PPG 7[40]. However, unlike a National Park boundary, the Heritage Area boundary is not permanent because it is defined through the local plan process. This has led to piecemeal review and amendment (notably at the New Forest District (East) Local Plan Inquiry in 1992, the Test Valley Borough Local Plan Inquiry in 1993, and the New Forest District Local Plan Inquiry in 1997).

1996

After extensive public consultation, the New Forest Committee

confirmed its preferred boundaries for the New Forest Heritage Area in February. These boundaries were used as the basic point of reference throughout ERM's National Park boundary study for the Countryside Agency in 2000. (There are small but significant differences between the boundary recommended by LUC in 1991, that confirmed by the New Forest Committee in 1996, and that defined in current local plans for the area.)

1998

As part of its advice to Government on protected areas[41], the Countryside Commission recommended that the New Forest be formally designated as a National Park. The reasons included:
- to give the area a permanent boundary;
- to ensure planning protection fully comparable to National Parks;
- to establish a statutory Authority;
- to require the preparation of a statutory management plan;
- to provide the Authority with secure government resources to carry out its functions;
- to facilitate adequate support for land managers for measures necessary to conserve the Forest – these include commoning in recognition of its role in maintaining the New Forest landscape.

The Commission advised that designating the New Forest as a National Park could be justified against the criteria of the 1949 Act. However, tailor-made legislation was identified as the preferred route to designation because of the special circumstances in the New Forest, particularly the statutory duties of the Verderers and the Forestry Commission under the New Forest Acts.

29 September 1999

The Government announced that it was asking the Countryside Agency to consider the designation of the New Forest as a National Park under existing legislation. While recognising the potential advantages of designation through tailor-made legislation, the Government did not wish to pursue this option[42].

October 1999

The Countryside Agency decided to begin the process of designating the New Forest as a National Park under the 1949 Act. It commissioned consultants ERM to carry out a study to advise the Agency when it was identifying the boundary.

42. Letter to the Countryside Agency from the Rt Hon Michael Meacher, Minister for the Environment, 29 September, 1999.

Appendix C

The New Forest National Park boundary study: methodology

The Countryside Agency commissioned a study from consultants Environmental Resources Management (ERM) to give technical advice on identifying a draft New Forest National Park boundary. This consultation document draws extensively on ERM's report.

The brief

The main objective of the study was to provide technical advice for identifying a boundary for the New Forest National Park based on National Park purposes and boundary setting conventions.

It looked at an area which included the New Forest Heritage Area and the South Hampshire Coast Area of Outstanding Natural Beauty (AONB). The New Forest Heritage Area is already recognised by Government as having similar planning status to a National Park. The South Hampshire Coast AONB, much of which lies within the Heritage Area, is an attractive coastal landscape which has strong historical links with the New Forest and its land management system.

The study included reviewing work carried out in 1991[43] to define the New Forest Heritage Area Boundary, testing that boundary against National Park criteria (see Chapter 2), considering if other areas should be included within a National Park boundary, and advising on the inclusion of essential backup grazing land and on the threats to the New Forest landscape character.

Approach

The boundary study started in December 1999. It was steered by the Countryside Agency, with information and advice from a technical working group of officers drawn from district and county councils, the New Forest Committee, the New Forest Verderers and English Nature.

Stage one was a desk review of New Forest character, including sources such as The New Forest Landscape[44], The New Forest District Landscape Character Assessment[45] and a wide range of reference books about the New Forest's landscape, wildlife, historical and cultural character. The aim was to crystallise out the key characteristics of the New Forest, highlighting what typifies the area, and what distinguishes it from surrounding landscapes. This work helped to define the 'area of search' for a National Park boundary.

ERM also reviewed National Park legislation and designation practice, exploring in some detail the National Park criteria and their interpretation. This review, carried out in close consultation with senior staff at the Countryside Agency, led to development and refinement of the methodology for defining a National Park boundary.

43. Land Use Consultants, New Forest Heritage Area: Proposed Boundary, report to the New Forest Committee, 1991.

44. Countryside Commission, The New Forest Landscape (CCP 220), Countryside Commission, 1986.

45. Environmental Resources Management, New Forest District Landscape Character Assessment, report to New Forest District Council, Hampshire County Council, The Countryside Agency and English Heritage, 2000.

The second stage of the study involved mapping and comparing the various boundaries for the New Forest Heritage Area, notably the 1991 Land Use Consultants boundary[46], the 1996 boundary as adopted by the New Forest Committee and endorsed by the Countryside Agency, and the current boundary as defined in adopted local plans. This was complemented by a field survey. ERM met local authority planning staff and reviewed development planning and development control issues, including the outcome of local plan public inquiries at which the Heritage Area boundary was considered. All the relevant structure plans, local plans and minerals and waste local plans were examined.

In relation to backup grazing, work was undertaken to establish the numbers and distribution of New Forest commoners and stock by parish. Changes in recent decades were assessed. Key boundary issues and 'areas in question' were identified for further study.

The team then carried out detailed research to assess whether different sections of a possible boundary met the National Park criteria. The research included a landscape field survey and analysis of aerial photographs; an analysis of the distribution of sites of wildlife, archaeological, historic, built environment and recreational interest; and a study of the distribution of existing and potential backup grazing land.

An iterative process was used to appraise the merits of particular boundary areas. It drew on desk research; expert opinion from members of the team, the technical working group and others; a landscape field survey and analysis of aerial photographs; analysis of the patterns of nature conservation and historical interest; and a study of land with potential for backup grazing.

Relatively early on the team began to distinguish two main sorts of area:

- where the Heritage Area (or AONB) boundary generally meets the National Park criteria and has stood the test of time in planning terms;
- where major changes in the boundary should be considered, termed 'areas in question'.

Although all areas of the boundary were examined closely, the study focused on the 'areas in question', carrying out more detailed landscape field survey and backup grazing research for these. For each of the 'areas in question' a series of boundary options was developed and their relative merits were explored and tested through desk and field survey.

Detailed boundary recommendations were then prepared.

Landscape assessment

One of the most difficult and contentious areas in identifying National Park and AONB boundaries has always been the definition of 'natural beauty'. In the 1980s and 1990s the

46. Land Use Consultants, New Forest Heritage Area: Proposed Boundary, report to the New Forest Committee, 1991.

Table 6.
Definitions of landscape character and landscape quality

Landscape character is:

what makes one landscape different from another. It means the distinct and recognisable pattern of elements that occurs consistently in a particular type of landscape. Distinctive character results from particular combinations of geology, landform, soils, vegetation, land use, field patterns and human settlement. It creates the particular sense of place of different parts of the landscape.

Landscape quality is:

a function of the extent to which the character of a landscape type is demonstrated in a particular area, in terms of the presence of key characteristics and the absence of atypical or incongruous features. It also depends upon the state of repair of elements in the landscape and the integrity or intactness of the landscape.

47. Countryside Commission, Landscape Assessment: A Countryside Commission Approach (CCD 18), Countryside Commission, 1987.

48. Countryside Commission, Landscape Assessment Guidance, Countryside Commission, 1993.

49. Land Use Consultants and Department of Landscape University of Sheffield, Interim Landscape Character Assessment Guidance, report to the Countryside Agency and Scottish Natural Heritage, 1999.

Countryside Agency and its predecessor body, the Countryside Commission, published a number of landscape assessment guidance documents that help to define 'natural beauty' and the related concepts of 'landscape character' and 'landscape quality' – all of which are relevant to boundary definition.

The first document in this series was Landscape Assessment: A Countryside Commission Approach, published in 1987[47]. This explored the meaning of natural beauty in the context of National Park management, saying that "the factors which are significant for the Commission's work in considering natural beauty are many and varied". A long checklist of factors affecting natural beauty included:

- physiographic (defined as geology, soils, land form, land use, vegetation, habitats, wildlife, archaeology and artefacts);
- aesthetic;
- historical and cultural;
- intangibles, such as feelings evoked in the observer;
- public accessibility.

This definition was elaborated in the 1993 Landscape Assessment Guidance[48] which stated that: "in addition to the scenic or visual dimension of landscape, there is a whole range of other dimensions, including geology, topography, soils, ecology, archaeology, landscape history, land use, architecture, and cultural associations. All of these factors have influenced the formation of the landscape, and continue to affect the way in which it is experienced and valued. Cherished landscapes can be said to have a natural beauty. The term embraces all of the dimensions of the landscape listed above, and also implies that the landscape is more than the sum of its component parts."

The more recent Interim Landscape Character Assessment Guidance[49] sets out definitions of landscape character and quality, shown in Table 6.

The Interim Guidance also gives advice on criteria which can be used in identifying valued landscapes. These include assessing landscape as a resource; landscape quality; scenic quality; consensus; conservation interests; other factors such as wilderness qualities. These provide useful background and additional definitions.

Appendix D
The New Forest – natural beauty

As explained in Chapter 3, in order to define a draft boundary the natural beauty of the potential New Forest National Park area was assessed in terms of landscape, ecology, history and commoning. This appendix describes each of these aspects in detail.

Landscape

'Natural beauty' is inextricably bound up with landscape character. This is especially true in the New Forest, where natural beauty is closely related to its particular range of landscape types[50].

The landscape types on which the draft New Forest National Park boundary are based are taken from the New Forest District Landscape Character Assessment. The classification is more detailed than, but consistent with, that used in the 1991 New Forest Heritage Area Boundary study.

Within the Forest core
- ancient and ornamental woodland
- timber inclosure/plantations
- heathland

Around the edge of the Forest core
- heath associated estates
- heath associated smallholdings and dwellings
- ancient forest farmlands

Coastal landscapes
- coastal fringe
- coastal plain estates: small parliamentary enclosures
- coastal plain estates: large informal enclosures

River valley landscapes
- river terrace farmlands
- river floodplain
- enclosed valley sides
- small scale enclosed valley

Other landscape types
- urban areas
- industrial areas (including gravel/mineral extraction, heavy industry, Fawley Refinery complex)
- historic parkland

Non-Forest landscapes
- enclosed farmland and woodland
- enclosed arable farmland
- open arable downs
- heathland scrub mosaic
- chalk river valley
- scarps
- lowland small scale mixed farmland

50. Land Use Consultants, New Forest Heritage Area: Proposed Boundary, report to the New Forest Committee, 1991.

All these except the last group are typical New Forest landscape types. The peripheral types of landscape are clearly different from those of the New Forest, particularly the arable, downland and other chalk landscapes in the north and west of the area looked at.

All the typical New Forest landscapes fall within the New Forest Countryside Character Area[51] and share a number of key characteristics:

- historically they were an integral part of the New Forest system of land management, with its complex mosaic of woodland, heathland, grassland and farmland landscapes;
- they have ancient features – not only woodland, heathland, ancient enclosures and settlements, but also ancient drove roads that link the enclosed landscapes to the adjoining open forest;
- they are still characterised by commoning influences, including grazing animals, and the associated traditional smallholdings.

The New Forest landscapes are easily distinguished from those of adjoining areas. To the east, the South Hampshire Lowlands Countryside Character Area is a mainly pastoral landscape of small, irregular fields and woodlands on rich deep soils. To the west, the Dorset Heaths Character Area shares a similar geology to the New Forest, but is a larger-scale, more sparsely populated landscape with extensive conifer plantations. To the north, the Salisbury Plain and the West Wiltshire Downs Character Area is an extensive, open, rolling chalk plateau dominated by large arable fields.

Table 7, which is an extract from the New Forest District Landscape Character Assessment[52] summarises the key characteristics and features of each of the principal types of landscape within and adjacent to the New Forest.

According to the Countryside Agency's approach to drawing National Park boundaries (see Table 2) unsightly development, such as industrial landscapes (heavy industry and Fawley Refinery complex) should generally be excluded from the National Park, and certain other types such as urban areas and where there is gravel/mineral extraction need to be carefully evaluated.

The landscape characteristics described in Table 7 provide a yardstick for judging the quality of a landscape and whether it should be included within the National Park. The obvious types of landscape to consider for inclusion are the river terrace farmlands and river floodplain of the Avon valley, plus parts of the coastal fringe and coastal plain estates. Substantial areas of all of these types are excluded from the New Forest Heritage Area.

51. Countryside Agency, Countryside Character Volume 7, The South East and London (CA 13), Countryside Agency 1999

52. Environmental Resources Management, New Forest District Landscape Character Assessment, report to New Forest District Council, Hampshire County Council, The Countryside Agency and English Nature, 2000,

Table 7.
Types of landscape

Landscape types	Description
Forest core	
Ancient and ornamental woodland	Ancient unenclosed oak and beech woods forming the heart of the ancient landscape of the New Forest. This landscape originated in the 18th century or earlier from wood-pasture. The woodlands generally take the form of beech and oak with an understorey of holly, with birch, thorns, yew and grassy glades. Secondary expansions of ancient and ornamental woods including pinewoods, birchwoods and holly groves. Riparian woods of alder and sallow are also included in this category.
Timber Inclosures /plantations	Within the perambulation, woodland stands behind fences within statutory inclosures. These inclosures have been managed for the production of wood and may be plantation oak or beech dating from 1800, mixed oak or beech plantations dating from 1810, mixed plantations of conifers with oak and beech or conifer plantations. Conifer plantations occupy just over half the total area of the inclosures. The ornamental drives, which contain many ornamental and exotic species, are a feature of this type.
Heathland	Heathland areas that arise on poor acid soils. The heathland is typically a mosaic of wet bogs, bracken, gorse, and tracts of heather which supports particularly important habitats and vegetation types, many of which are internationally rare or threatened species and some of which are included on Annex I of the EU Habitats Directive. These heaths are characterised by long views across the open heath; Scots Pines rise out of the plain singly or in clumps, their sculptural forms punctuating the skyline. Settlement tends to be confined to the margins of the heath.
Forest edge	
Heath associated smallholdings and dwellings	A variable, small-scale pastoral landscape with a regular field pattern defined by ditches and banks, often fringed with gorse or hedgerows and gapped up with fencing or tin sheeting. The area has developed from relatively recent enclosure from former common and is characterised by a heathy character, lack of mature trees and low quality pasture, often used as back-up grazing land for commoners' stock. Linear roadside settlements and associated smallholdings have arisen from progressive encroachment.
Heath associated estates	An enclosed wooded estate landscape, often on undulating ground, around the fringe of the forest. This landscape is closely associated assiated with a zone of former heathland and still retains a heathy character; pine and oak plantations are interspersed by tracts of open heath and intensively farmed land consisting of large fields enclosed by hedgerows and woodland edges. There are few settlements or roads.
Ancient forest farmlands	A farmed forest landscape with a strong sense of enclosure and an ancient irregular enclosure pattern. Ancient woodlands are a feature of the landscape and create a feeling of being 'in the forest'. A network of winding leafy lanes and drove roads with roadside oaks and wide verges links small areas of remnant wayside common. There are scattered farmsteads and occasional roadside cottages of brick, timber and thatch.

Landscape types	Description

Coastal

Coastal plain estates – small parliamentary enclosures	An intensively farmed, but well managed landscape of small regular fields with straight boundaries formed by, or linked to, the parliamentary enclosures of the late 18th – early 19th century. Fields are divided by hedgerows; hedgerow oaks are a feature. These and the remnants of ancient woodland provide visual links to the Forest. A number of small river valleys drain south into the Solent. Traditional built forms are scattered brick and tile farmsteads, and country houses with estate cottages and gatehouses. Weatherboarding is a feature on agricultural buildings.
Coastal plain estates – large informal enclosures	An intensively farmed, but well managed, large scale estate landscape with both informal enclosures dating from the late medieval period and the 17th – 18th century, and more regular 18th – 19th century parliamentary enclosures. Fields are divided by hedgerows with hedgerow oaks. Blocks of ancient woodland and recent plantations lend a wooded character and small wooded river valleys drain south into the Solent. Again, brick and tile farmsteads, weatherboarded outbuildings and large country houses with estate cottages and gatehouses are traditional built features. There are clear views over the Solent to the Isle of Wight.
Coastal fringe	A large scale, flat, open landscape with wide views and a quiet, but exposed and bleak character. Saltmarsh, shingle beaches, muddy creeks, grazing marshes and coastal woodlands are features supporting waders, wildfowl and other birds. A series of coastal forts, including Calshot Castle and Hurst Castle, lines the coast. Wooded skylines form a backdrop and contrast to the open shoreline.

River valley

River terrace farmlands	A flat, open, intensively farmed landscape with a medium to large scale regular field pattern resulting from 18th and 19th century parliamentary enclosures. Fields are bounded by low-cut hedgerows or tree belts, often of pine. The landscape is largely open with long views to the distant woods and heaths. Settlement is confined to scattered farms and occasional clusters of dwellings along communication routes; larger built up areas occur at historic crossing points.
River floodplain	A flat, low-lying pastoral river landscape, frequently associated with former water meadows. Water, both in the river channel itself and in any associated drainage ditches, is an important landscape element. Meandering river channels are bordered by gently sloping grazed banks beyond which lies an open landscape of meadows and rough grazing. Individual floodplain trees stand out as features.
Enclosed valley sides	This landscape type is an extension of the enclosed valley sides landscape type defined in the Test Valley Borough Landscape Assessment. It is described as a flat low-lying predominantly pastoral landscape of meadows, pasture and arable farmland with a remote, riparian character. The enclosed valley floor is charact-erised by a dense network of hedgerows and trees.

Landscape types	Description
Other types	
Historic parkland	Parkland landscapes which are designed landscapes often associated with a large house and sited to take advantage of views. They are characterised by historic connections and landscape features such as scattered trees, rows of trees, wood pasture (in the case of deer parks), exotic trees, ancient pollard trees and veteran trees. Substantial woodlands and shelter belts are also features of these designed landscapes.
Urban areas	Dense urban areas which are not an integral part of the surrounding landscape, as a result of their size or form, have been given a separate category. They tend to be large settlements which are inward looking towards a town centre and which have a large area of residential development around their core which acts as a barrier between the town centre and surrounding landscape.
Gravel/mineral extraction	Large scale gravel pits, particularly in the Avon valley, which are now water-filled and function as recreational lakes. These gravel pits are often surrounded by trees and are therefore not visible, although the signs advertising their recreational functions are often clues to their presence.
Heavy industry	Discrete areas in which industrial structures dominate the landscape. These areas are found primarily along Southampton Water and often result in substantial impacts on visual amenity.
Fawley Refinery complex	A large industrial oil refinery site which is strongly enclosed by functional screen planting which obscures views into the site. However, the multitude of stacks and flares of the refinery protrude above the top of the tree line, and as such the refinery site has a large visual influence over the surrounding area. The original grain of the landscape, including field patterns and settlement patterns, has been obscured.
Non-New Forest landscape	
Enclosed farmland and woodland	A wooded agricultural landscape, often on undulating terrain, forming the boundary with the chalklands. Mixed arable (on drier ridges) and grazing land (in clayey hollows) of medium irregularly shaped fields. Ancient semi-natural woodlands, hedgerows with hedgebanks and hedgerow trees create a strong sense of enclosure. Diverse habitats include streams, water meadows, commons and some ancient field systems. Network of winding lanes links scattered farmsteads and villages which are often associated with village greens.
Enclosed arable farmland	Eroded dip slope margins of chalk at the edge of the transition to lowland clays. A landscape of farmland, numerous semi-natural ancient woodlands (including oak-hazel coppice) and hedgerows with hedgerow oaks creating a strong sense of enclosure. Historically the rounded bluffs provided defensible sites for hill-forts and several of the hills are crowned with ramparts. The pattern of settlement is distinctive; linear villages lie within valleys.

Landscape types	Description
Open arable downs	Landscape dominated by arable farmland in a broad open setting – typically a pattern of large regular fields divided by low, fragmented, treeless hedgerows or post and wire fencing. Remnant downland clings to the steeper hill slopes. The area has low woodland cover; hill top copses mark archaeological sites and plantations and shelterbelts provide functional windbreaks. Apart from isolated clusters of farm buildings, settlements are generally on lower ground and within valleys. Ancient drove roads, boundary earthworks and visible archaeological features demonstrate the historic importance of this landscape.
Chalk down scarps	Tracts of unenclosed downland survive on the steeper scarp slopes of the chalklands providing a striking contrast to the adjacent enclosed farmland. The scarps often form prominent ridgelines and also provide vantage points with panoramic views. The species-rich calcareous grassland has great nature conservation value and is managed by grazing. Many of these scarps are the sites of ancient hill forts and the extent of visible archaeology is exceptional.

Ecological considerations

The nature conservation character and interest of the area looked at is described in the New Forest Natural Area Profile[53]. This supports the idea of a broad definition of New Forest landscapes, encompassing not only the Crown lands but also the coast and the Avon valley.

The Crown lands are at the core of the Natural Area. They include the open grazed Forest of heathland, wood pasture and Forest lawns. They also include the silvicultural inclosures from which stock are generally excluded. Today open grazing by commoners' stock is confined to the perambulation, using cattle grids and fencing.

However, according to the New Forest Natural Area Profile: "The Natural Area extends beyond the perambulation to incorporate the Avon valley to the west, much of the coastal plain between Christchurch and Calshot spit to the south and the urban fringe of Southampton Water, known as the waterside, which borders the Natural Area to the east. For much of its history, the pastoral economy of the open forest relied upon this much wider area to support the commoners' stock. Evidence of these links occurs throughout the Natural Area in the form of old drove roads, linear commons and greens."

There are a number of habitat types in the area. Core areas of woodland, heathland and lawn are ringed by a wide belt of predominantly arable land, within which there are many small woodlands and pockets of grassland. The grassland, which often functions as backup grazing for commoners' stock, is largely concentrated in coastal areas (along the waterside and south of

53. English Nature Hampshire and Isle of Wight Team, New Forest Natural Area Profile, English Nature, 1998.

Lymington) and in the Avon valley where there are extensive areas of flood meadow.

Table 8 gives the three main areas where the key features of nature conservation interest are found.

Outside these three areas, the wider countryside also contains many important semi-natural habitats. These include fragmented areas of lowland heath (particularly in the west), enclosed meadows, former wood pasture, ancient coppice woodlands and many agriculturally unimproved grasslands. Wide, tightly-grazed grassy verges are a feature of both the enclosed and unenclosed roads in the open forest, with commoners' stock roaming widely along enclosed country lanes.

Table 8.
Key features of nature conservation interest

Forest core

Within the Forest core (the Crown lands, commons and manorial wastes) there are large areas of four types of habitat that are now fragmented and rare in lowland western Europe:

- lowland heathland
- valley and seepage step mires
- acid to neutral grasslands, including Forest lawns and greens
- ancient wood pasture.

Coast

Important physical features include:

- river gravel terraces, whose coastal exposures along the Solent are nationally important
- coastal sedimentary features, such as shingle spits and saltmarshes.

Habitat features include:

- fine examples of coastal grazing marshes and saltmarshes (eg. between Hurst Spit and the Lymington River)
- saline lagoons
- shingle features which support vegetation
- intertidal mudflats.

Avon valley

In the Avon valley:

- the floodplain grasslands are nationally-important habitat for waders, wildfowl and invertebrates
- there are important areas of acid grassland on the gravel terraces above.

There are a number of sites of national and international importance for nature conservation within the area looked at. Wide areas are of European and international importance under the EC Habitat Directive and Birds Directive, and the Ramsar International Convention for the protection of wetlands. The New Forest core has been designated as a candidate Special Area of Conservation (cSAC), a Special Protection Area (SPA) and Ramsar site because it contains habitat types and/or species which are threatened in a European context. Much of the Solent and Southampton Water are designated as a candidate SAC, an SPA, and a Ramsar site because of their coastal habitat and importance for birds. The Avon valley from Christchurch to Bickerton, which includes a wide range of river valley and wetland habitats and is important for breeding and wintering birds, is designated as an SPA and a Ramsar site. The river is also a candidate SAC for its full length.

In addition to these designations there are several Sites of Special Scientific Interest (SSSI) that are of national nature conservation importance. The whole river floodplain extending north into Wiltshire is also part of the Avon Valley Environmentally Sensitive Area (ESA).

Both the habitat character and the distribution of sites of nature conservation interest have influenced the drafting of a boundary for the National Park. In accordance with the Agency's

approach to drawing National Park boundaries (Table 2), wherever practicable the draft boundary includes features of national nature conservation importance which are on the margins of the National Park.

Historical considerations

The area's archaeological, historical, cultural, architectural and vernacular character and qualities are all relevant considerations in identifying a National Park boundary. The historic landscape character of the New Forest is described in the New Forest Landscape Character Assessment[54], the Hampshire Historic Landscape Assessment[55], and the New Forest Archaeological/Historical Landscape Character Assessment[56].

The history of human settlement of the New Forest dates back to at the least the Bronze Age when the land was largely cleared of its primeval forest, becoming infertile and able to support only heathland. On pockets of richer soils within the Forest and all around the edge, ancient woodland survived and settled farming communities were established by local woodland clearance, a process known as assarting. The Royal Hunting Forest, established in 1079, formalised this situation. Key elements have survived to the present day in the form of rights of common, which allow the surrounding communities access to Forest resources. The Court of Verderers administers the

54. Environmental Resources Management, New Forest District Landscape Character Assessment, report to New Forest District Council, Hampshire County Council, The Countryside Agency and English Heritage, 2000.

55. Oxford Archaeological Unit and Scott Wilson, Hampshire Historic Landscape Assessment, report to Hampshire County Council and English Heritage, 1999.

56. Wessex Archaeology, The New Forest Archaeological/Historical Landscape Character Assessment, report to the New Forest Committee, 1996.

commoning system.

These basic historic landscape patterns have been in place for a thousand years or more. The farmed landscapes around the edge of the Forest are inextricably linked to the Forest core because they have long been part of the same management system. Before the New Forest Act of 1964, which led to fencing the perambulation and the installation of cattle grids, stock was allowed to roam over a wide area. This extended as far as Totton, Hythe, Lymington, Ringwood and Fordingbridge. Grazing animals were therefore characteristic throughout most of the area considered in the boundary appraisal. The differences between the landscapes inside and outside the perambulation boundary were less pronounced than they are today.

The core of the Forest is dominated by open heathland with old woodland, most of which is heathland wood pasture or old enclosures. Smaller heathland commons occur around the western and northern edges of the main heathland block, next to settlements in the neighbouring river valleys, notably the Avon.

All around the margins of the Forest the landscape is dominated by small pre-parliamentary and parliamentary field patterns, together with recent urban settlement and, in coastal areas, horticulture and intertidal mudflats. In the Avon valley, west of the New Forest, there is a distinctive river terrace historic landscape. This is characterised by an extensive area of irregular rectilinear small-scale parliamentary enclosure fields, below which lie unimproved grassland and water meadows. This area is also characterised by old settlements beside the river. There are subtle changes in character within the valley. In particular, the fields tend to be larger and more regular in the south than in the north as a result of post-medieval rationalisation.

The surviving domestic architecture of the New Forest also shows variations that reflect the relative wealth and access to resources of different population groups. Cob (a mixture of earth and straw) was the traditional structural material, used for the houses of working people on the estates or on the Crown common land. Most freehold dwellings – especially along the Solent coast and the western edge of the Forest – were built of brick with timber frames. These patterns can still be seen today.

The unique historical and cultural status of the New Forest is widely recognised. The UK Government has proposed to the World Heritage Convention that the Forest should be a World Heritage Site on the grounds that it is an area of outstanding wildlife and landscape interest, fashioned by human intervention and use over thousands of years. The proposed World Heritage site description[57] refers to the area's rich archaeological heritage, particularly Bronze Age and

57. Department for Culture, Media and Sport, World Heritage Sites: The Tentative List of the United Kingdom of Great Britain and Northern Ireland, Department for Culture, Media and Sport, 1999.

Roman, and its documented history which goes back to the 11th century.

Formal common rights were established by the mid-16th century. The quality of the habitats and landscapes of the New Forest is acknowledged as being dependent on the exercise of common rights and the continued existence of a small community of active commoners who make up a distinct social group. The visual and historical continuity and the shared history of the Forest core and the more fertile areas around the periphery are highlighted as key qualities of the historical and cultural landscape.

The area includes many Scheduled Ancient Monuments, sites on the English Heritage Register of Historic Parks and Gardens, and Conservation Areas (all designations of national importance)[58]. There are also many other sites of archaeological, historical and architectural interest. Where practicable, important sites around the margins of the area have been included within the draft National Park boundary. This has influenced the line, particularly south of Lymington and in the Avon valley where there are a number of Conservation Areas.

Commoning considerations

The traditional commoning system of land management remains a key feature of the New Forest's rural economy and community life. It is also of crucial importance to the

landscape and ecological character of the Forest and to the continuance of that character[59].

No other area of Britain has such large areas of Crown land subject to common rights administered by a body set up by statute (The Verderers).

Commoning has been an important consideration when identifying a draft boundary. Land with rights to forest and common grazing occurs both within the Forest perambulation and in the broad fringe of countryside around the periphery, extending fairly continuously along the waterside, the Solent coast and the Avon valley, as well as northwards into Wiltshire[60]. The rights are definitive, attached to the landholding, and cannot be extinguished even if they are not exercised.

Commoners are individuals who possess rights of common. They exercise their grazing rights by turning their stock out on the open forest (depasturing). Only a small number are able to make a complete living from commoning stock; most are part-time commoners supplementing their income from other sources. Others simply keep one or two animals on the Forest to maintain this age-old tradition.

It helps if commoners have access to 'backup grazing' to support their commoning activities. This land may be owned or rented. In recent years commoners have found it increasingly difficult to purchase suitable properties and small

58. Data provided by local authorities.

59. Further information on the commoning system and its evolution can be found in Countryside Commission, The New Forest Commoners (CCP 164), Countryside Commission, 1984 and Stagg, D and J Page, Two Reports on New Forest Commoning (CCD 45), Countryside Commission, 1989.

60. Stagg, D and Page, J, Two Reports on New Forest Commoning (CCD 45), Countryside Commission, 1989.

holdings because of very high prices – reflecting the area's popularity with commuters and holidaymakers. In addition, it has become very difficult to purchase or rent suitable paddocks or fields because of the premium values of such land for more intensive forms of agriculture, recreational horse-keeping and, in some cases, mineral extraction and urban development.

Against this background, and in order to assess the way in which commoning considerations should influence the National Park boundary, a review was carried out as part of the boundary study the Agency commissioned[61]. This review looked at:

- the current status of the commoning system, including the total number of commoners and stock, and their distribution by parish: this indicates the areas where commoning is most active;
- trends within the commoning system over the last 30 years, including in particular parishes, and threats to the system that may be relevant to identifying the boundary;
- backup grazing, including its current distribution, the potential of land around the Forest to provide additional backup grazing, and the relative levels of need in different areas.

The review showed that in 1999 there were 441 practising commoners – the highest figure recorded over the 30-year period – in a total of 41 parish units around the Forest, turning out a total of 6,763 ponies and cattle (of which 3,878, ie. 57 per cent, were ponies and 2,885 were cattle)[62]. In terms of numbers of commoners the parishes with the greatest number form a semi-circle around the west and south of the Forest. In terms of numbers of stock turned out, the picture is slightly different: Bramshaw is by far the most important parish, followed by Beaulieu and Hyde. However, more than 200 stock are turned out in each of the peripheral parishes of Copythorne; Fawley; Boldre; Hordle; Sopley; Ellingham, Harbridge and Ibsley; and Fordingbridge. The 18 'core' parishes that each have in excess of 100 animals account for approximately 80 per cent of the practising commoners and 85 per cent of the stock turned out.

Tables 9 and 10 show that there were high numbers of both commoners and stock in the 1970s, comparable with 1999 numbers. However, during the 1980s the number of commoners declined to 334. There were parallel declines in stock numbers, first cattle and then ponies. The late 1980s and early 1990s then saw a fairly steady rise in numbers of commoners and stock, with a general increase in numbers of cattle relative to ponies.

Specific local trends during the 1990s were:

- substantial increases in cattle numbers (but not in numbers of commoners) in the parishes of Fordingbridge and Sopley in the Avon valley - here there are

61. Specialist input to the study in relation to commoning and backup grazing was provided by Joanne Way (nee Page). The full findings are presented in two working papers submitted to the Countryside Agency.

62. Figures are based on data supplied to Joanne Way by David Stagg, originally taken from marking fee registers.

some very large individual cattle herds, held by small numbers of commoners;

• substantial increases in both numbers of commoners and numbers of stock in the parishes of Beaulieu and Hordle.

The reasons for these changes are poorly understood, but the increase in numbers of commoners and stock during the 1990s is attributed at least in part to cattle and pony premium schemes[63]. The underlying economic environment for commoning appears to be rather poor. There are a number of problems facing commoners which have been identified in various reports on the subject.[64 65 66 67] Among the inter-related issues highlighted in these reports are:

• poor levels of return from commoning, with heavy reliance upon Forestry Commission Pony and Cattle Premium Schemes to maintain incomes from commoning;

• concerns that the supply of affordable backup grazing land may be inadequate, particularly as a result of the competing demands of recreational horse-keeping;

• the poor market for Forest ponies, partly because the commoning system offers little scope for rearing or holding foals off the Forest (which in turn adversely affects their quality and marketability as 'ready to ride' ponies);

• significant decline in the total agricultural land area (-8 per

Table 9.

Trends in number of commoners for 18 'core' parishes, 1978–1999

Parish	1978	1982	1988	1999
Bramshaw	39	41	40	38
Beaulieu	5	12	11	28
Hyde	13	20	18	24
Boldre	26	29	19	28
Denny	12	6	6	18
Fordingbridge	5	9	8	10
Hordle	4	1	1	11
Copythorne	17	20	16	18
East Boldre	32	30	27	32
Fawley	23	28	17	27
Brockenhurst & Rhinefield	19	23	23	25
Ellingham, Harbridge, Ibsley	24	23	19	24
Sopley	2	2	2	2
Sway	13	12	10	10
Totton & Eling	15	10	15	16
Minstead	16	10	13	14
Burley	29	24	13	22
Ringwood	11	10	7	8

63. ADAS, Management of Agricultural Land Within the New Forest Heritage Area, report to the New Forest Committee, 1993.

64. ADAS, Management of Agricultural Land Within the New Forest Heritage Area, report to the New Forest Committee, 1993.

65. ADAS Consulting Limited, Verderers' LIFE Project: The Marketing of New Forest Livestock, report to The Verderers, 1998.

66. Cox, G et al, Recreational Use of Horses in the New Forest Heritage Area, report to the New Forest Committee, 1994.

67. FRCA, Agricultural Census Data for 1988-1998: New Forest Heritage Area, unpublished data produced on behalf of MAFF.

Table 10.
Trends in total stock numbers for 18 'core' parishes, 1978–1999

Parish	1978	1982	1988	1999	% of total stock which are ponies
Bramshaw	981	929	938	819	61
Beaulieu	57	105	149	621	47
Hyde	358	353	385	517	60
Boldre	193	125	189	352	70
Denny	623	292	260	352	40
Fordingbridge	29	56	62	348	19
Hordle	60	1	20	334	45
Copythorne	326	314	322	332	71
East Boldre	504	457	392	309	80
Fawley	127	192	202	303	72
Brockenhurst & Rhinefield	175	196	160	240	62
Ellingham, Harbridge, Ibsley	385	243	188	232	53
Sopley	17	30	42	202	2
Sway	161	117	135	182	61
Totton & Eling	108	90	103	174	80
Minstead	184	125	236	157	86
Burley	218	203	148	150	62
Ringwood	73	74	49	135	73

cent) and in areas of grassland (-14 per cent) and rough grazing (-25 per cent) in the New Forest Heritage Area between 1988 and 1998;

• the potential importance of the ESA meadowlands in the Avon valley to increase the availability of grassland and hence meet essential backup grazing needs.

In addition, there is some concern that the supply of open grazing land in the Forest has diminished over the years[68]. In particular, the fencing of the Forest perambulation in the 1960s resulted in a loss of open grazing. This was because many of the adjoining and satellite commons, grazing marshes and associated network of droveways, verges and greens became isolated from the open forest[69]. The introduction in the 1960s of legislation requiring the registration of commons may also have contributed to the loss of open grazing. Traditionally, under the system of 'vicinage', adjacent commons and marshes were grazed in conjunction with the open forest, with animals moving freely along drove roads between the two. However this system effectively ended when the perambulation was fenced. In addition, some people have argued[70] that including some adjacent commons within the perambulation encouraged the decline of commoning in areas

68. A study of loss of grazing in the New Forest is currently being undertaken by Jonathan Cox and Richard Reeves for Hampshire Wildlife Trust, the Commoners' Defence Association and the New Forest Association.

69. The introduction in the 1960s of legislation requiring the registration of commons may also have contributed to the loss of open grazing.

70. New Forest District East Local Plan Inquiry, evidence of Captain Timothy Elliot Moore, 1992.

such as the Avon valley between Ibsley and Fordingbridge. This was because commoners had to pay marking fees for the first time.

One option that has been suggested to counter the loss of open grazing is to allow stock to roam outside the perambulation once again, for example on suitable areas of common land and roadside verges. It is argued that there could be benefits both for nature conservation and for the landscape because grazing would enhance the sense of being in the New Forest.

A key issue in identifying a draft boundary was how to take account of the long-term needs and sustainability of the commoning system. The principal aim was to include within the National Park an adequate supply of land (affordable for commoners to own or rent) which could serve as backup grazing. A secondary consideration was to include areas that were formerly grazed in conjunction with the open forest.

There has been lengthy – and often inconclusive – debate in the past about the definition of an adequate supply of backup grazing. The subject was addressed by ADAS in its 1993 report[71] but has also been examined at a number of local plan inquiries. As part of its boundary study, ERM carried out qualitative desk research and structured interviews with key people in the Forest with personal knowledge and experience of commoning and grazing issues. This research

explored the geographic distribution of:
- land currently/recently used for backup grazing[72];
- land potentially suited to backup grazing, ie. grassland and other land of low agricultural quality that commoners could afford;
- the level of need for backup grazing, given that such grazing is usually located within 5 km, at most, of the commoner's holding[73].

The findings of this work were used to help identify a draft National Park boundary.

71. ADAS, Management of Agricultural Land Within the New Forest Heritage Area, report to the New Forest Committee, 1993.

72. The approximate distribution of practising commoners' holdings and backup grazing land in 1988 was mapped by Joanne Page. This map was used by Land Use Consultants in defining the Heritage Area boundary and also formed a reference source for ERM's study. A copy is lodged with the Verderers.

73. Land Use Consultants, New Forest Heritage Area Proposed Boundary, report to the New Forest Committee, 1991.

Appendix E

The New Forest – open air recreation and public enjoyment

The New Forest's general ability to meet the second statutory criterian for designation of a National Park – opportunities for open–air recreation is widely recognised, as discussed within Chapter 3.

The New Forest Landscape, CCP 220[74] is an important point of reference. Citing the reasons why the landscape of the New Forest is so important, this report highlights the fact that it is an outstanding landscape for recreation. It has intrinsic appeal and is highly accessible. There is unhindered access on foot to open land through the accepted privilege of open access to enjoy 'air and exercise' on Crown land, and excellent provision for its enjoyment. The value of the landscape for recreation is reflected in the high number of visitors, equivalent to most National Parks.

To this can be added the considerable recreational importance of the South Hampshire AONB. The Solent coast is internationally recognised for sailing and boating. It is the longest stretch of unspoilt coastline on England's south-east coast.

A key feature of the New Forest is what it offers in terms of recreation. Many visitors go there because it is one of the few remaining extensive quiet rural areas in the crowded and highly urbanised south-east of England.

Research by the University of Portsmouth[75] shows that the top four reasons for visiting the New Forest are scenery, ease of access, peace and quiet, and to see the animals.

The most recent estimates indicate that the New Forest receives in the region of 7 million day visits per year[76]. However, research by the University of Portsmouth in 1996 has shown that this figure may underestimate the number of visits to the Forest made by local people (possibly accounting for up to 18 million per year)[77].

Around 40 per cent of visits are by holidaymakers; 30 per cent by local residents; and 30 per cent by day visitors from elsewhere[78].

The New Forest fulfils a particular role for local communities in the waterside parishes and the southern coastal towns. The majority of the area's day visitors come from Southampton and Bournemouth/Poole and it is estimated that 15 million people live within day trip range.

Once in the Forest, visitors – especially holiday makers – take part in a range of activities, especially countryside ones. Some go simply to view the Forest or coastal scenery, but many take part in active pursuits. Of these walking is by far the most popular, undertaken by around half of all visitors. Other activities

74. Countryside Commission, The New Forest Landscape (CCP 220), Countryside Commission, 1986.

75. Land Management Research Unit of the University of Portsmouth, The New Forest Sport and Recreation Study, The New Forest Committee, 1996.

76. Ecotec Research and Consulting Limited, Tourism in the New Forest 1991-92, report on the tourism survey to the New Forest District Council, Southern Tourist Board and New Forest Tourism, 1992.

77. Forestry Commission, Enjoying the Forest - Recreation 2000. An access and recreation plan for the Crown Lands of the New Forest. Consultation draft. Forestry Commission, July 2000.

78. Ecotec Research and Consulting Limited, Tourism in the New Forest 1991-92, report on the tourism survey to the New Forest District Council, Southern Tourist Board and New Forest Tourism, 1992.

in order of popularity are dog walking, picnicking, camping and caravanning, cycling and horse riding[79].

In addition, sailing, angling and other coastal pursuits are very popular along the waterside, but particularly within the Solent. These activities are mainly serviced from Hythe, Calshot, Bucklers Hard, and Lymington. Many thousands of people sail for pleasure in the Solent and Southampton Water. These are amongst the most popular sailing waters in the world, and the coastal landscape makes a substantial contribution to the quality of the experience. Lepe Country Park on the Solent Coast attracts over 500,000 visitors a year.

There is accommodation for holidaymakers throughout the Forest, which is nationally renowned for its camping and self-catering accommodation. Hotels and guest houses tend to be concentrated in the larger centres, notably Brockenhurst, Lyndhurst, Lymington, Beaulieu and Burley. These, as well as the peripheral towns of Milford-on-Sea, Ringwood and Fordingbridge, provide the main services and facilities for visitors.

The New Forest Committee's document, A Strategy for the New Forest[80], and other more recent reports[81] highlight the pressures on the New Forest in terms of damage to its fragile landscapes and habitats, commoning system and potential for quiet enjoyment. They encourage measures such as:

- co-ordinating the recreation strategy of the coast and the Forest;
- moving car parks, camping sites and visitor centres away from sensitive areas to more robust areas on the Forest fringe;
- using the Solent Way and the Avon Valley Path as alternatives to walking in the Open Forest;
- integrating the rights of way network of the enclosed landscapes with that of the central parts of the New Forest to reduce erosion by walkers and riders and to encourage local residents to visit on foot rather than by car;
- developing new attractions, such as country parks, outside the Forest to help direct pressure away from core areas.

They also recognise the potential recreational role of areas such as the coastal marshes at Lymington and Keyhaven, and the Avon valley's tranquil flood meadows and wetlands within former gravel workings. These offer valuable additional opportunities for quiet enjoyment, birdwatching, studying local history, and so on, within easy reach of urban populations.

The New Forest is already outstanding for recreation, especially on the Crown land, with its open access rights, and on the Solent Coast. There are many opportunities for understanding and enjoying the area's special qualities. However, one of the greatest challenges is how to resolve the conflict between recreational demand and conservation of the very resource that people come to experience.

The area's future potential for recreation will therefore depend on both improved management of existing recreational resources and the development of new opportunities for quiet open-air recreation. To optimise this potential and to protect the Forest's traditional quiet, pastoral character, the Forest core, the coast and the peripheral landscapes of the Forest need to be managed as a whole. The area proposed may offer new scope for meeting recreational needs in a sustainable way, especially those of local residents and day visitors, and alleviating pressures on the Forest core.

79. Land Management Research Unit of the University of Portsmouth, The New Forest Sport and Recreation Study, The New Forest Committee, 1996.

80. A Strategy for the New Forest - full working document, The New Forest Committee, February 1996.

81. Such as Environmental Resources Management, New Forest District Landscape Character Assessment, report to New Forest District Council, Hampshire County Council, The Countryside Agency and English Heritage, 2000, and the forthcoming Forestry Commission Visitor Management Strategy for the New Forest.

Appendix F
Glossary

For the purposes of this document, the following terms are defined as follows.

Adjacent commons – commons in a variety of ownerships outside the Crown land. Under the New Forest Act 1964, the adjacent commons were included within the boundary of the perambulation.

Area of Outstanding Natural Beauty (AONB) – AONBs are designated under the National Parks and Access to the Countryside Act, 1949. The primary purpose of designation is to conserve natural beauty.

Assart/assarted woodland – when human settlement began in the New Forest, the land was largely cleared of its primeval forest. It became infertile and heathland was formed. On pockets of richer soils, within and around the edge of the Forest, ancient woodland survived. The process known as assarting occurred when settled farming communities were established by local woodland clearance of these areas.

Backup grazing – enclosed pasture land that supports use of the Forest for common grazing. Generally it is located close to a commoner's holding. Its uses include overwintering of stock, raising store cattle, making hay or silage, tending sick animals and young stock, and preparing stock for market. In addition to the land that is in use as backup grazing at present, there is a wider pool of land currently used for other purposes that might be capable of use as backup grazing for future generations of commoners, subject to availability and cost.

Commons – areas of land, privately or publicly owned, which are subject to rights of common held by the commoners. The present perambulation of the New Forest (New Forest Act 1964) includes both common land owned by the Crown subject to Forest Rights, and privately owned adjacent commons and manorial wastes (see manorial greens) subject to common rights.

Commoners of the New Forest – individuals who exercise Forest and/or common rights. These rights are attached to certain properties. (See commons.)

Common rights – The new Forest Atlas of Common Rights was prepared under the 1949 Act – using the register of New Forest Claims published in 1858, and the 1964 Act extending the perambulation to include the adjacent commons. There are six different rights of common in the New Forest, of which common of pasture of commonable animals (ponies, horses, cattle and donkeys) and common of mast (pigs in the pannage season in autumn to collect acorns and beech nuts) are the most relevant today.

Conservation Area – Conservation Areas are established under Section 69 of the Planning (Listed Buildings and Conservation Areas) Act 1990, which imposes a duty on local planning authorities to designate as conservation areas, any "areas of special architectural or historic interest the character or appearance of which it is desirable to preserve or enhance".

Countryside Character Area/Natural Area – areas in England jointly defined by the Countryside Agency and English Nature which have a distinctive character.

Crown land – land owned by the Crown and vested in the Minister of Agriculture, Fisheries and Food. Crown land in the New Forest is managed on behalf of the Minister by the Forestry Commission.

Depasture – allow to graze. In the New Forest, the animals turned out to graze are known as 'the depastured stock'.

Enclosed land – fenced land from which commoners' stock are excluded, both in Crown and private ownership.

Environmentally Sensitive Area – ESAs are designed to help protect some of the most beautiful parts of the country from damage and loss that can come from agricultural change. The ESA schemes encourage farmers to adopt beneficial practices that will help to protect and enhance the environment of the designated area. They are designated and administered by the Ministry of Agriculture, Fisheries and Food.

Forestry Inclosure – See statutory inclosure.

Forest rights – these are rights of common arising from the Crown land. (See commons.) These are rights to use or harvest from the Forest (eg. turf, peat, furze, gravel, wood for building and burning, hunting etc) originating in the medieval period. Forest rights are registered in the 'Register of Decisions on Claims' 1858. Some Forest rights survive to the present and often overlap, or are reciprocal with common rights.

Manorial greens/wastes – during the medieval period land not in productive agricultural use was termed 'waste' and could belong to a manor or other land-holding. Such land was valuable, as it often contained useful natural resources including timber, turf, peat, plants for food or medicine, wild birds and animals, reed for thatching etc. It is now taken to be open, unenclosed and uncultivated land of a manor, subject to common rights.

New Forest Committee – an independent, non-statutory committee, co-ordinating the work of key Forest organisations which have responsibilities for the care of the Forest. Current members are: the Forestry Commission, the Countryside Agency, Verderers of the New Forest, Hampshire County Council, English Nature, New Forest District Council, Salisbury District Council, Wiltshire County Council, the Environment Agency. Observers are: the Country Landowners' Association, the National Farmers' Union, Test Valley Borough Council.

New Forest Heritage Area – the area which has planning policies as if it were a National Park. The boundary of the Heritage Area is defined through the local plan process.

Open Forest – unenclosed Crown land over which grazing takes place.

Parliamentary enclosure and pre-parliamentary enclosure – land 'enclosed' from the medieval common open fields into private ownership, often demarcated by hedges, occurring by private acts of parliament generally during the period of 'enclosure movement' 1750–1850. Similar enclosure occurred in earlier periods (pre-parliamentary) or during the 'enclosure movement' under private arrangements (parliamentary-type enclosure).

Perambulation – the historic term for the boundary of the area governed by Forest law, occasionally marked on the land, or otherwise in a charter, by an agent of the Crown literally walking (the act of perambulating) the boundary. It is defined in the New Forest Acts 1964 and encompasses Crown land, privately owned land, manorial wastes subject to common rights and privately owned enclosed land.

Ramsar site – a wetland of international importance especially for wildfowl, designated under the Ramsar Convention 1971 and listed under the Convention on Wetlands of International Importance.

Saltern – a plot of land used to produce salt by evaporating sea water in basins or troughs.

Seepage step mires – waterlogged areas where peat has been built up and bog plants grow.

Site of Importance for Nature Conservation (SINC) – non-statutory sites of local importance for nature conservation, identified by county councils and wildlife trusts.

Site of Special Scientific Interest (SSSI) – nationally important sites for nature conservation designated under the National Parks and Access to the Countryside Act 1949 and the Wildlife and Countryside Act 1981.

(Candidate) Special Area of Conservation (cSAC) – areas designated under the EC Directive on the Conservation of Natural Habitats and of Wild Fauna and Flora (The Habitats Directive) 1992 as being of European importance for habitats and species. Candidate SACs (cSACs) selected by the UK Government and submitted to the EU have the same protection under the Habitats Directive as SACs which have been formally designated.

Special Protection Area (SPA) – areas of European importance for birds, designated under the EC Directive on the Conservation of Wild Birds 1979 (the Wild Birds Directive).

Statutory inclosures – Crown land enclosed under earlier statutes and retained by the New Forest Act 1877 for the purpose of growing timber and trees.

Verderers of the New Forest – the Court of Verderers is a statutory body set up under the New Forest Act 1877. The jurisdiction of the Verderers extends over the area within the perambulation which is subject to the rights of pasture. Historically the Verderers have served as the representatives of the Crown with rights and duties for the routine administration of the Forest Rights. They have statutory duties and powers under the New Forest Acts for the protection and administration of the rights of common and of the health of the commoning animals.

Vicinage – this is a practice whereby an animal depastured on one common wanders on to an adjoining common or on to the open forest within the perambulation, all such land being subject to the rights of commoning stock.

Draft boundary maps

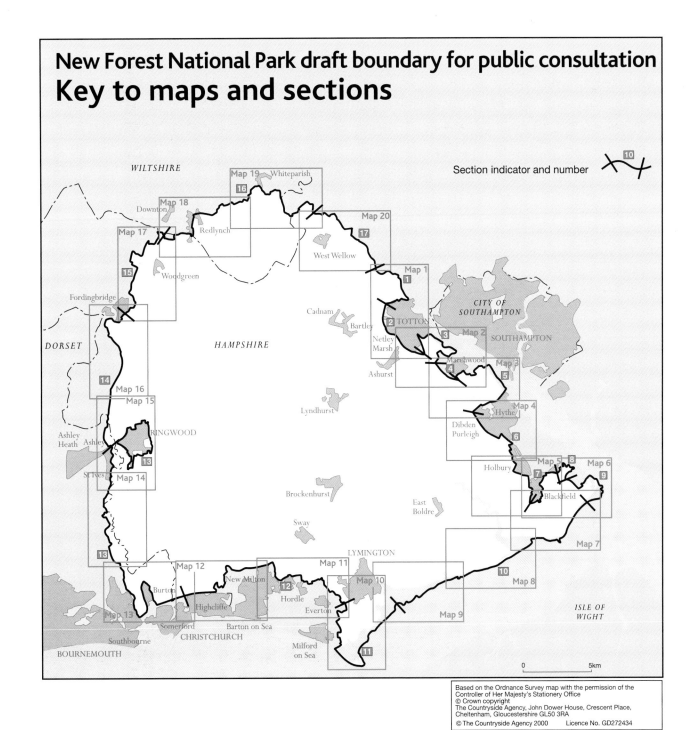

New Forest National Park draft boundary for public consultation
Key to maps and sections

Section indicator and number

WILTSHIRE

Map 19 Whiteparish
Map 18
Downton
Redlynch
Map 17
Woodgreen
West Wellow
Map 20

Map 1
CITY OF SOUTHAMPTON
Cadnam
Bartley TOTTON
SOUTHAMPTON
Netley Marsh
Map 2
Fordingbridge
Ashurst
Marchwood
Map 3
DORSET
HAMPSHIRE
Map 4
Hythe
Lyndhurst
Dibden Purlieu
Map 16
Map 15
RINGWOOD
Holbury
Map 5 Map 6
Ashley Heath Ashley
Blackfield
Map 13
St Ives
Map 14
Brockenhurst
East Boldre
Map 7
Sway
LYMINGTON
Map 11
Map 12
New Milton
Map 10
Map 8
Burton
Hordle
Everton
ISLE OF WIGHT
Highcliffe
Map 9
Map 13
Somerford
Barton on Sea
CHRISTCHURCH
Southbourne
Milford on Sea
BOURNEMOUTH

0   5km

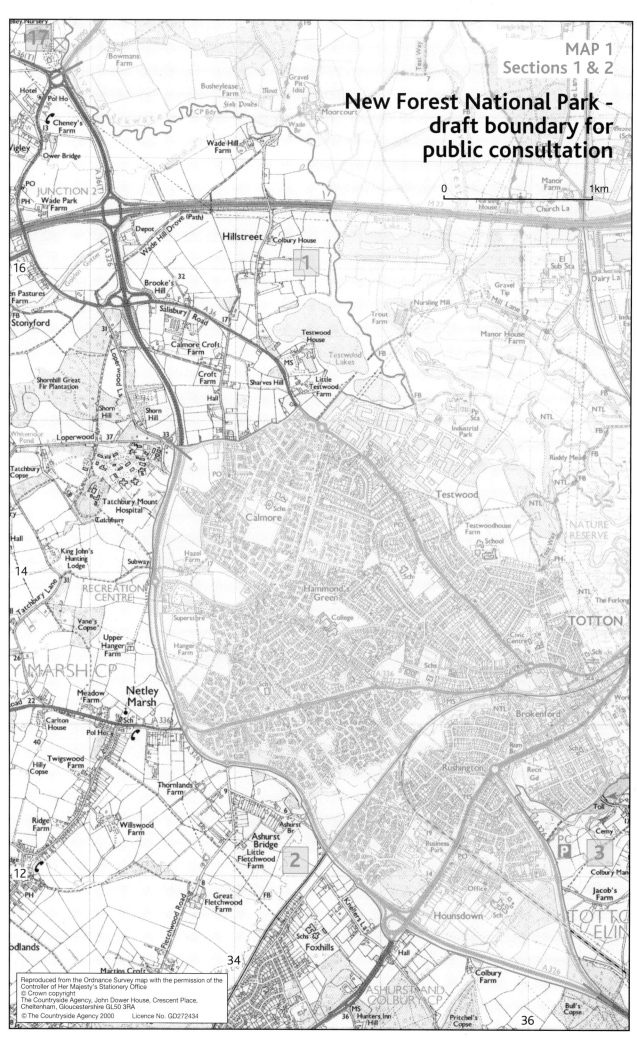

MAP 1
Sections 1 & 2

New Forest National Park - draft boundary for public consultation

0   1km

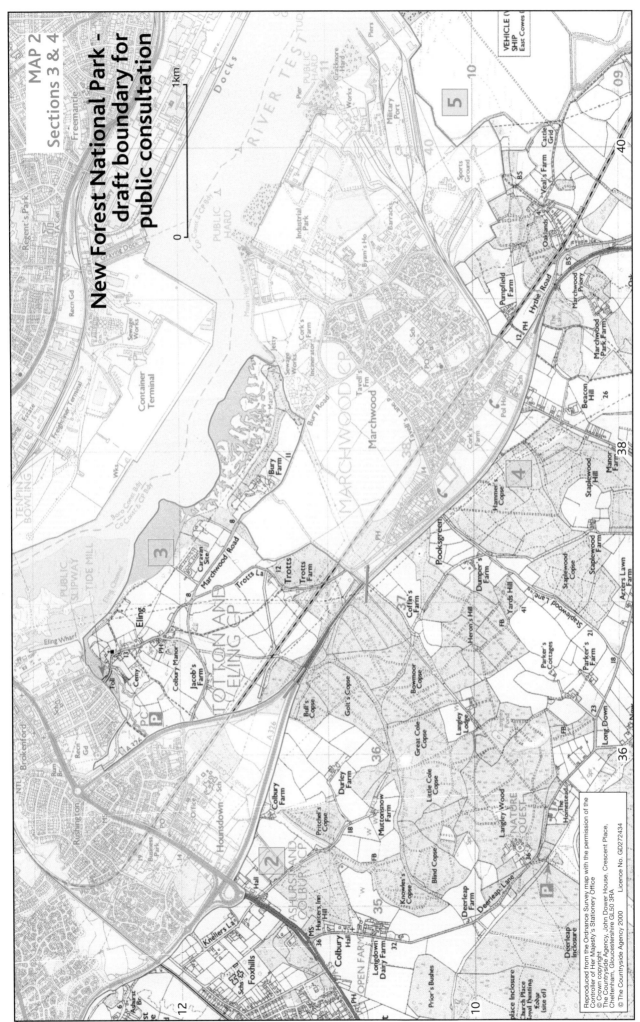

MAP 2
Sections 3 & 4

New Forest National Park – draft boundary for public consultation

0 _____ 1km

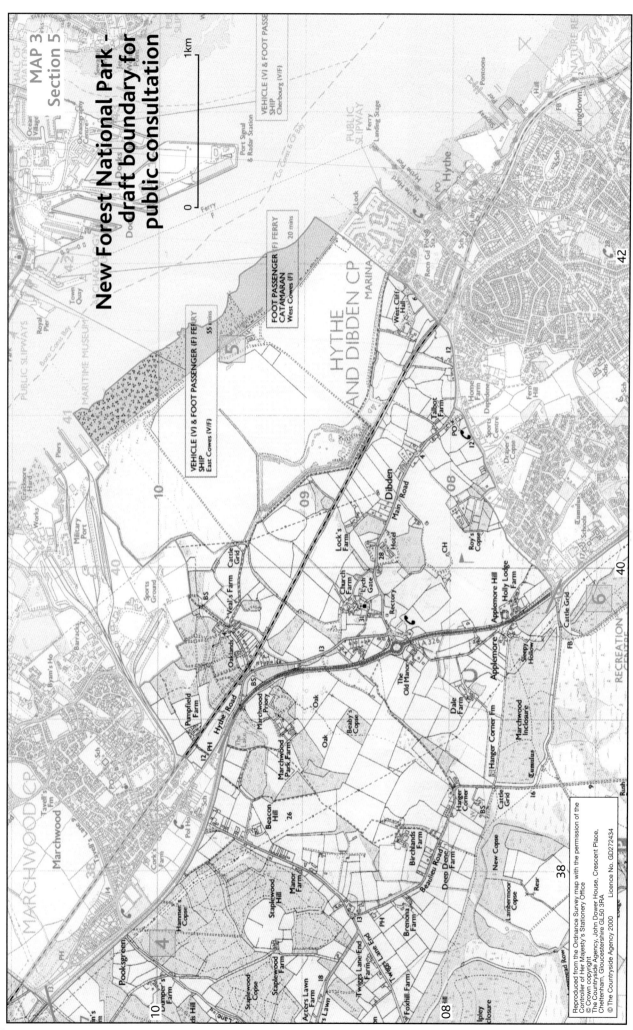

MAP 3 – Section 5

New Forest National Park –
draft boundary for public consultation

VEHICLE (V) & FOOT PASSE
SHIP
Cherbourg (V/F)

FOOT PASSENGER (F) FERRY
20 mins

VEHICLE (V) & FOOT PASSENGER (F) FERRY
55 mins

FOOT PASSENGER
CATAMARAN
West Cowes (F)

VEHICLE (V) & FOOT PASSENGER (F) FERRY
SHIP
East Cowes (V/F)

HYTHE AND DIBDEN CP

MARCHWOOD CP

0 _____ 1km

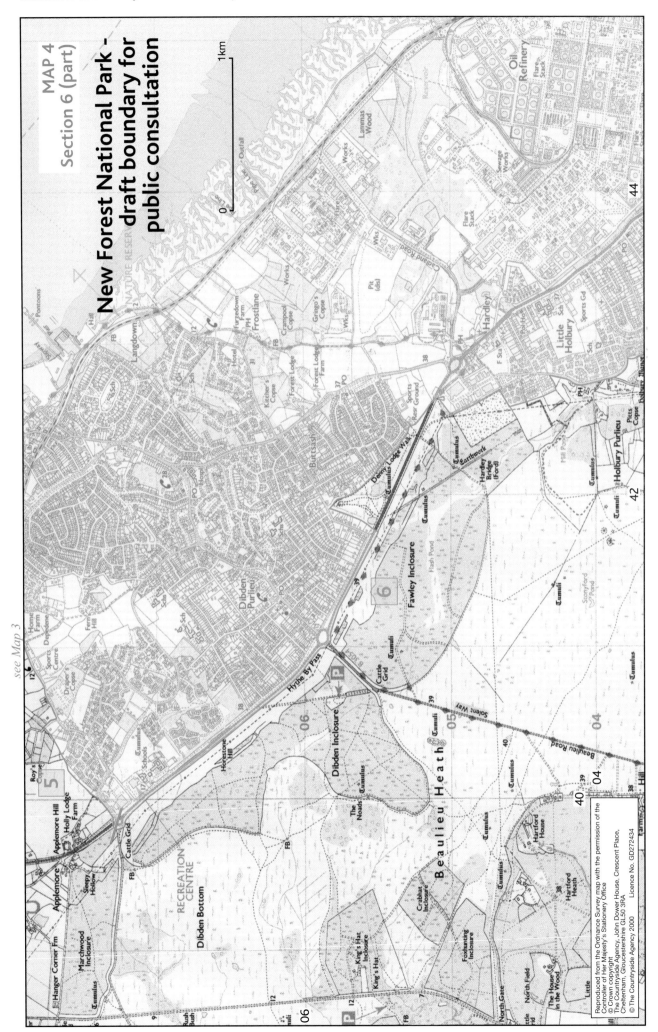

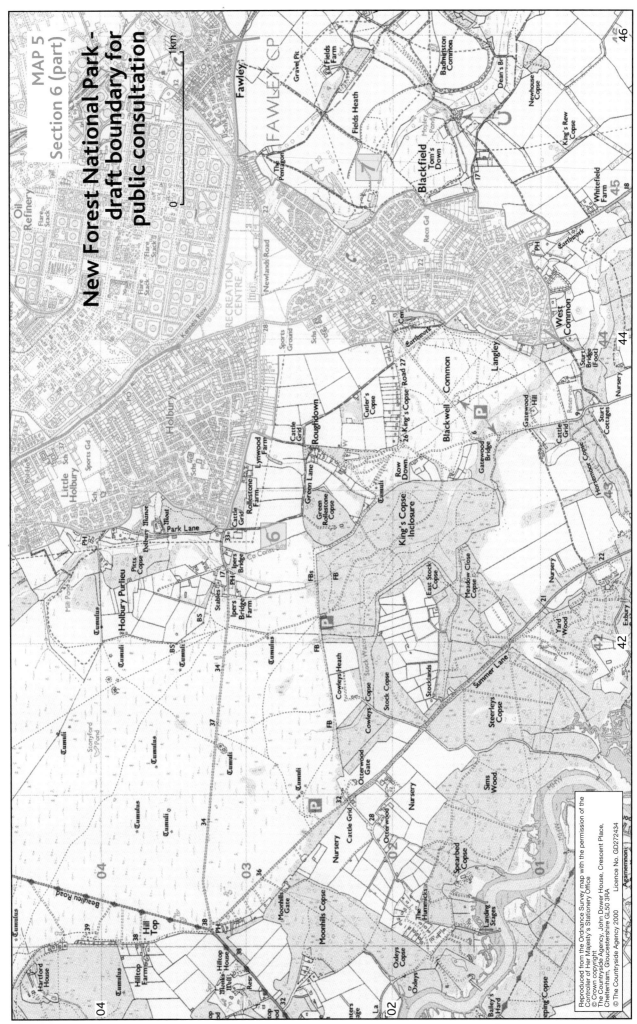

MAP 5
Section 6 (part)

New Forest National Park – draft boundary for public consultation

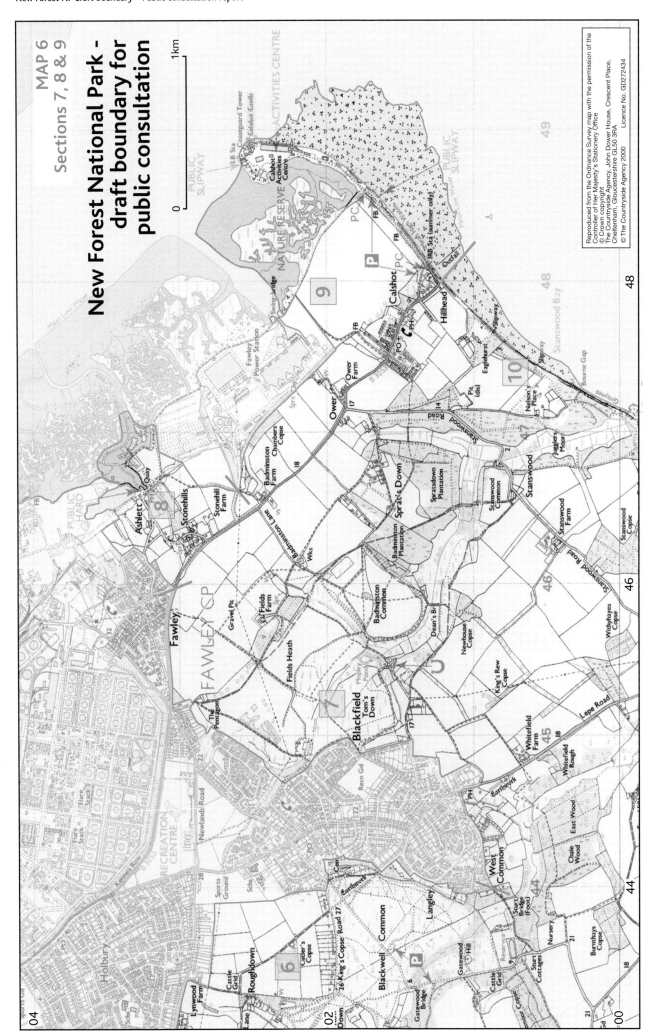

New Forest National Park –
draft boundary for
public consultation

MAP 6
Sections 7, 8 & 9

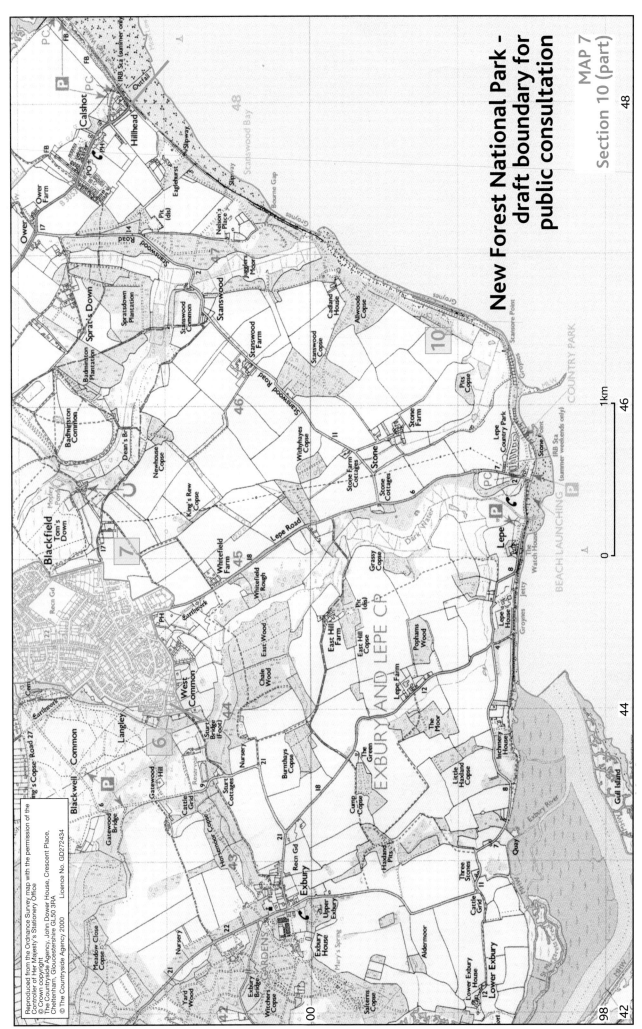

New Forest National Park - draft boundary for public consultation

MAP 7
Section 10 (part)

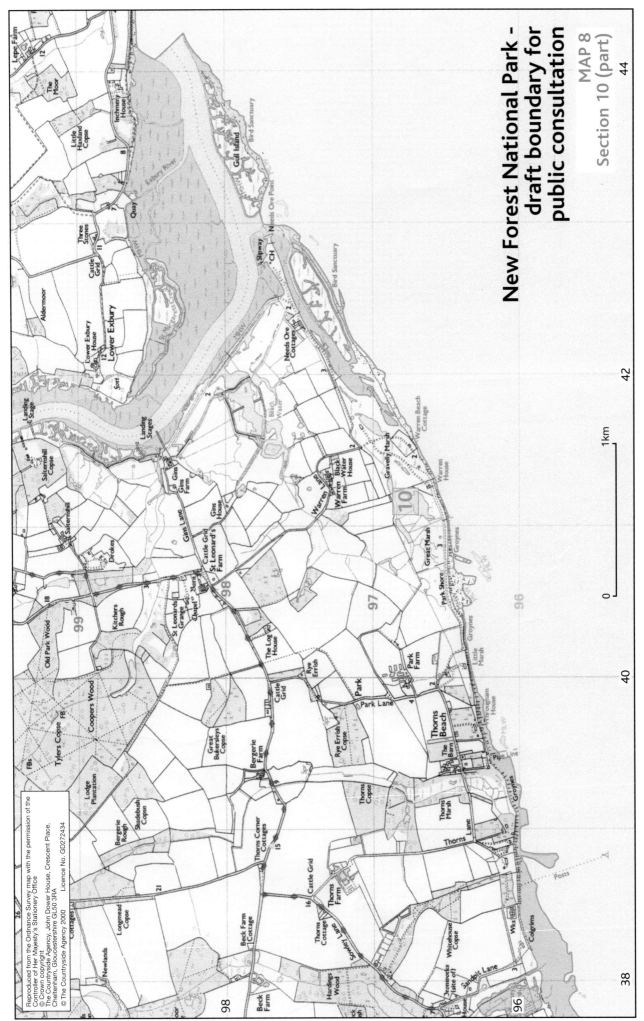

New Forest National Park –
draft boundary for
public consultation

MAP 8
Section 10 (part)

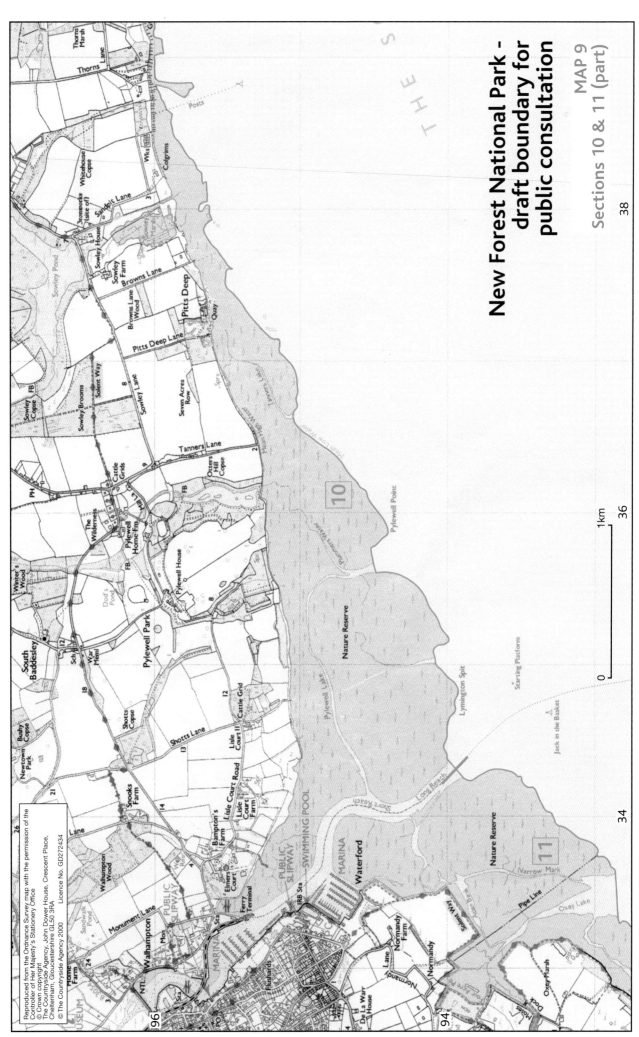

New Forest National Park -
draft boundary for
public consultation

MAP 9
Sections 10 & 11 (part)

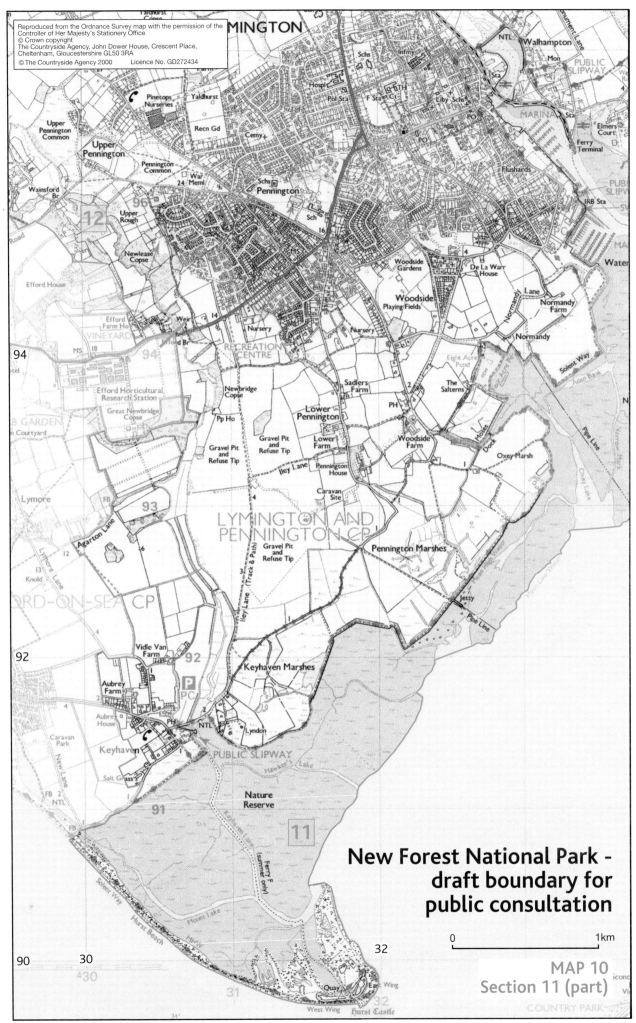

**New Forest National Park -
draft boundary for
public consultation**

0   1km

MAP 10
Section 11 (part)

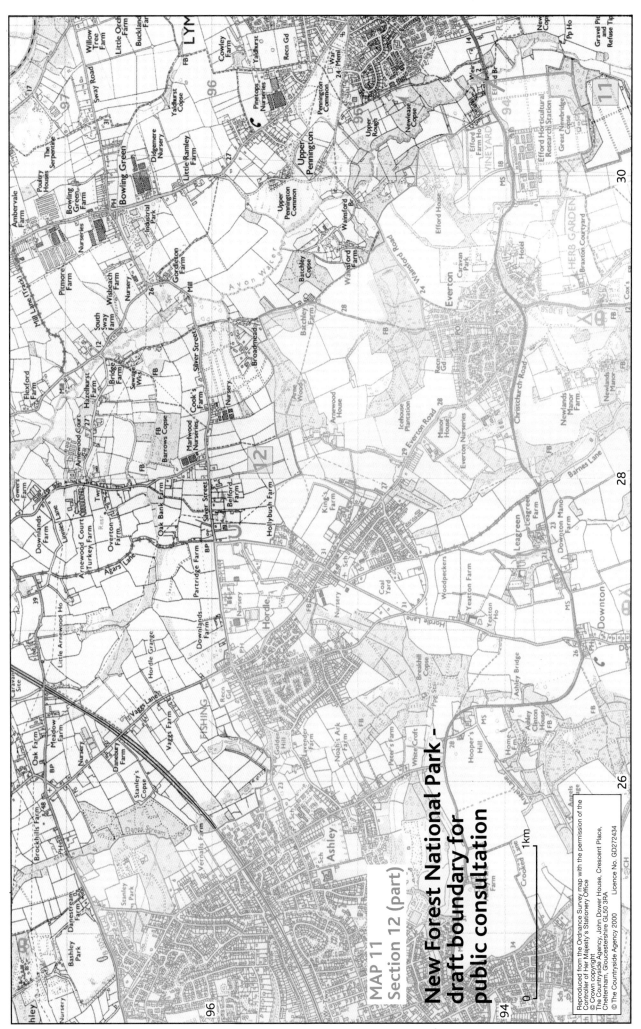

MAP 11
Section 12 (part)

New Forest National Park – draft boundary for public consultation

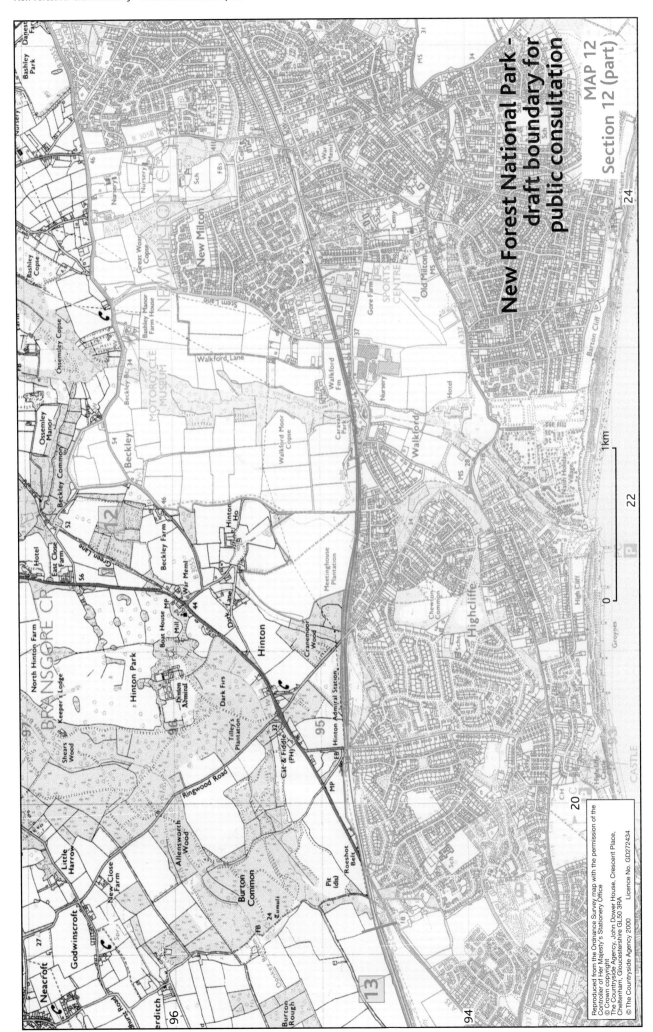

New Forest National Park –
draft boundary for
public consultation

MAP 12
Section 12 (part)

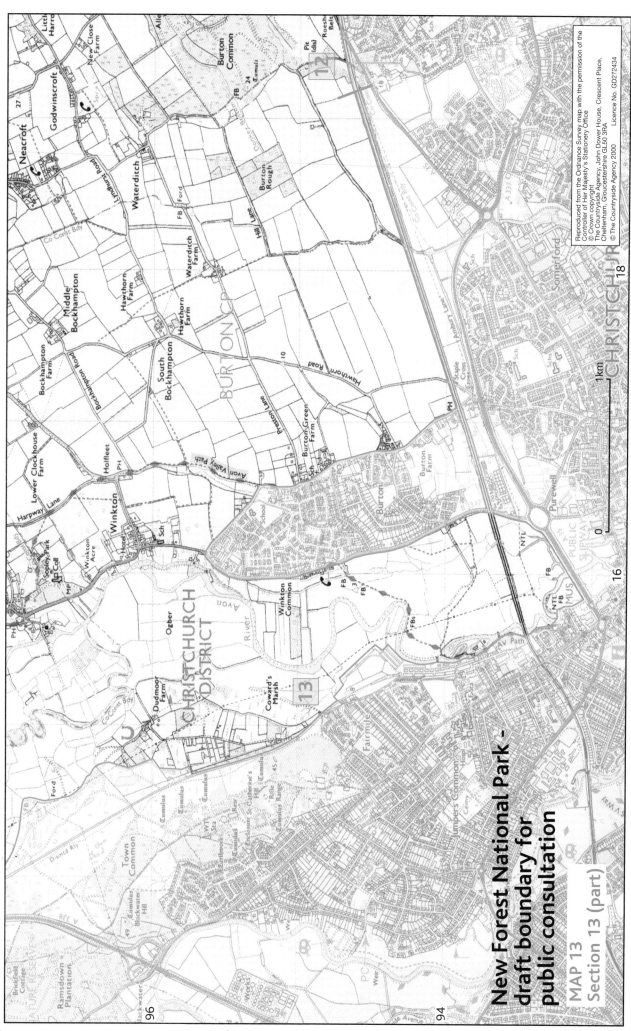

New Forest National Park –
draft boundary for
public consultation

MAP 13
Section 13 (part)

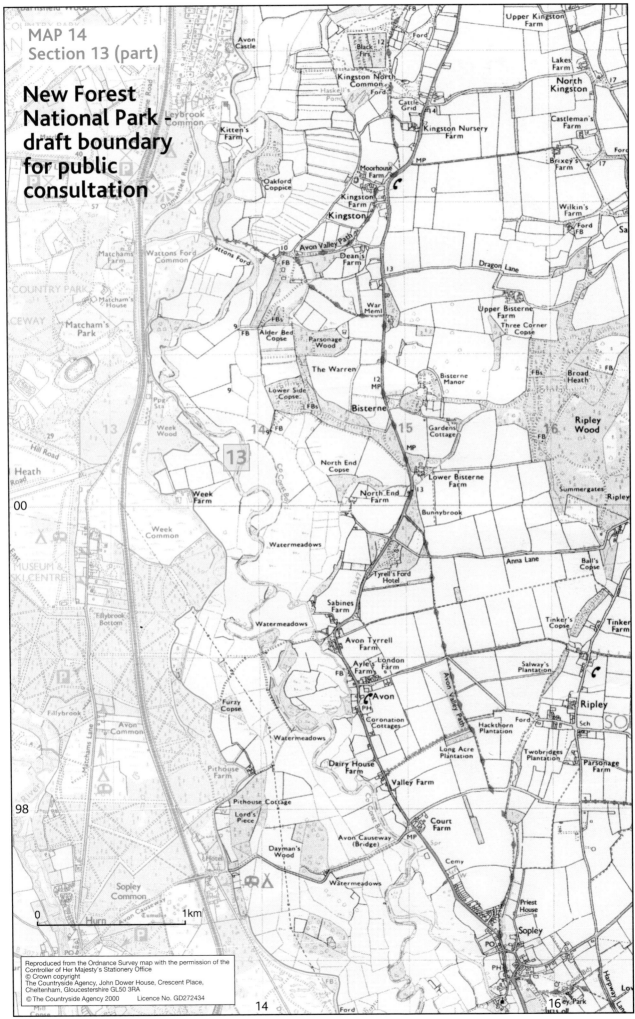

MAP 14
Section 13 (part)

New Forest National Park – draft boundary for public consultation

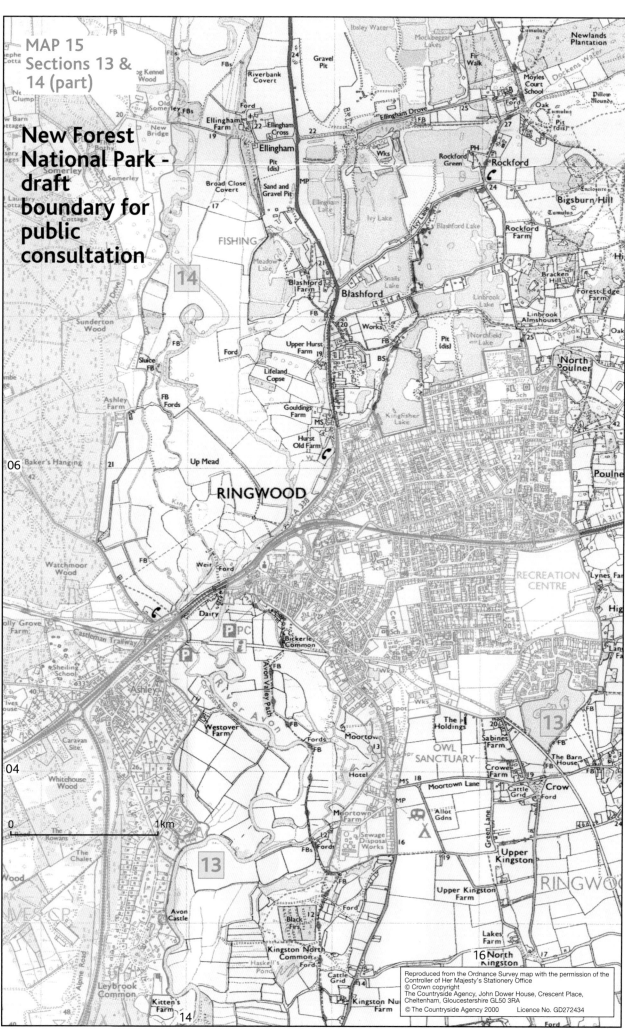

MAP 15
Sections 13 &
14 (part)

New Forest National Park – draft boundary for public consultation

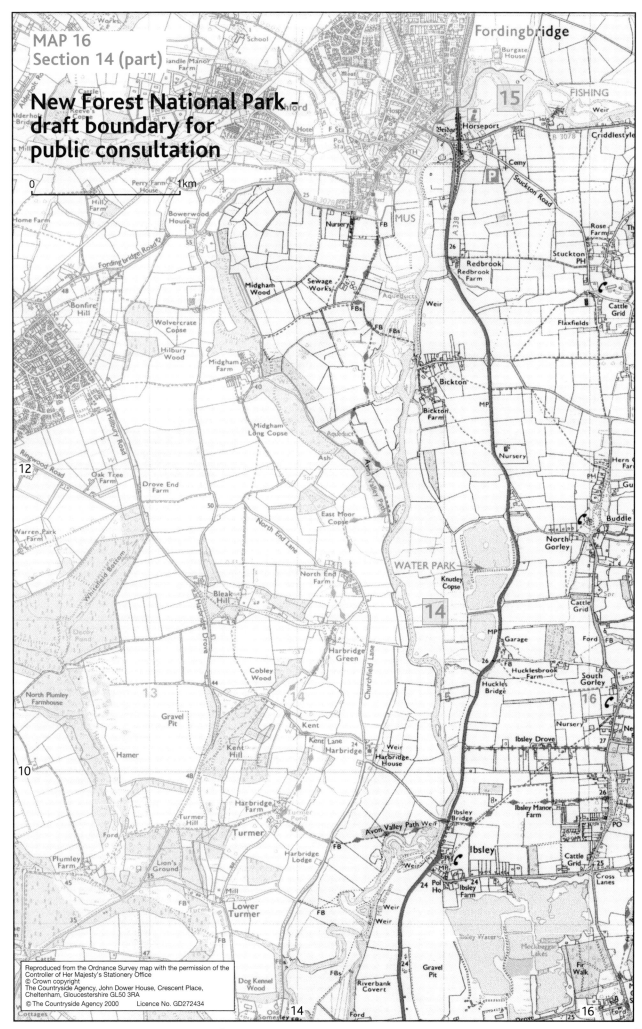

MAP 16
Section 14 (part)

New Forest National Park – draft boundary for public consultation

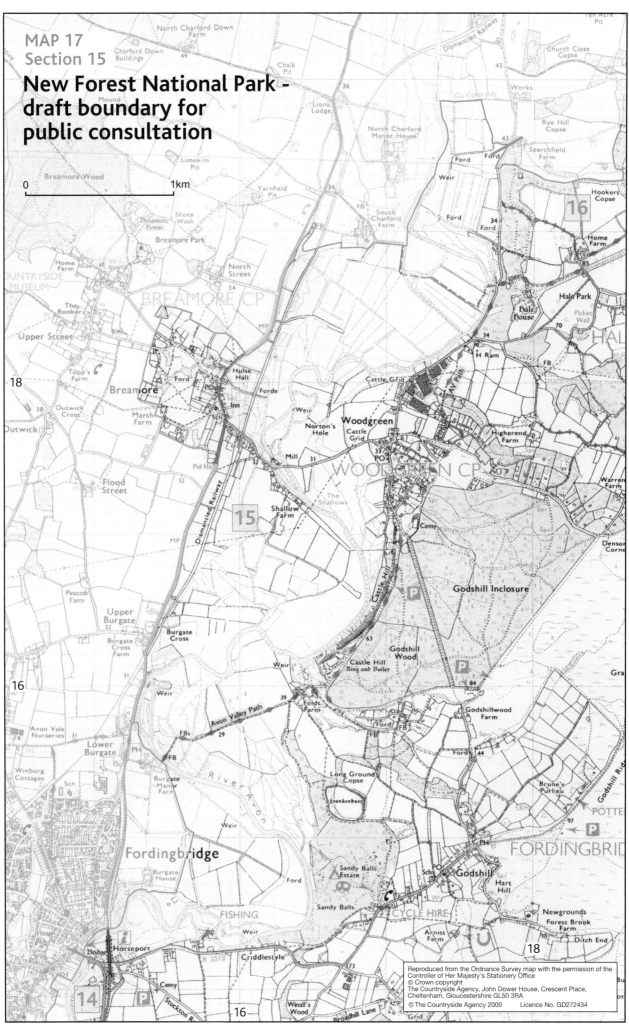

MAP 17
Section 15

New Forest National Park – draft boundary for public consultation

0   1km

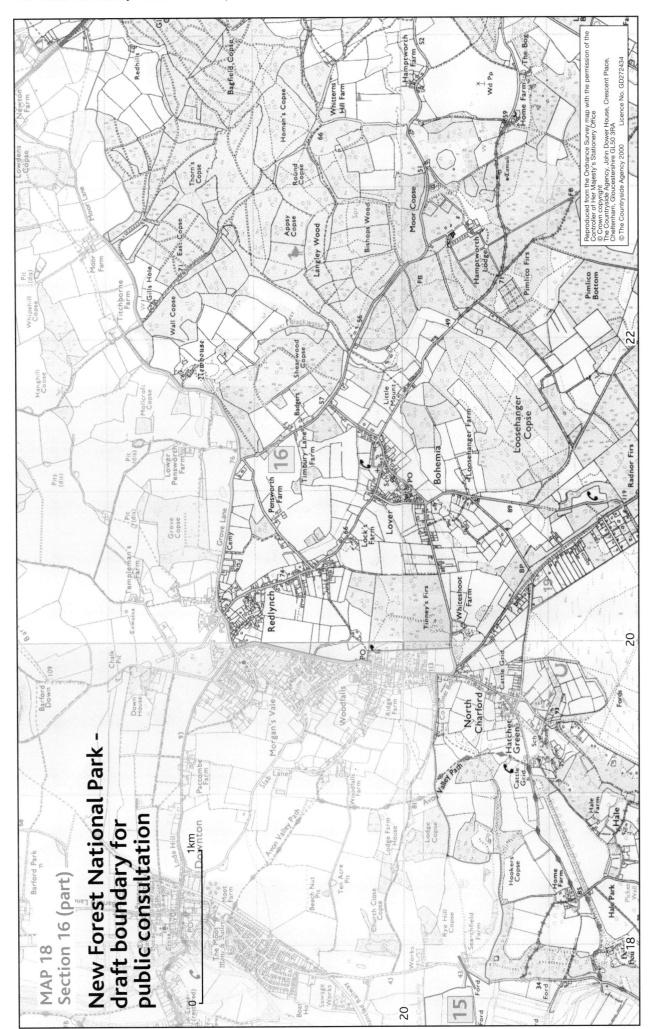

MAP 18
Section 16 (part)

New Forest National Park –
draft boundary for
public consultation

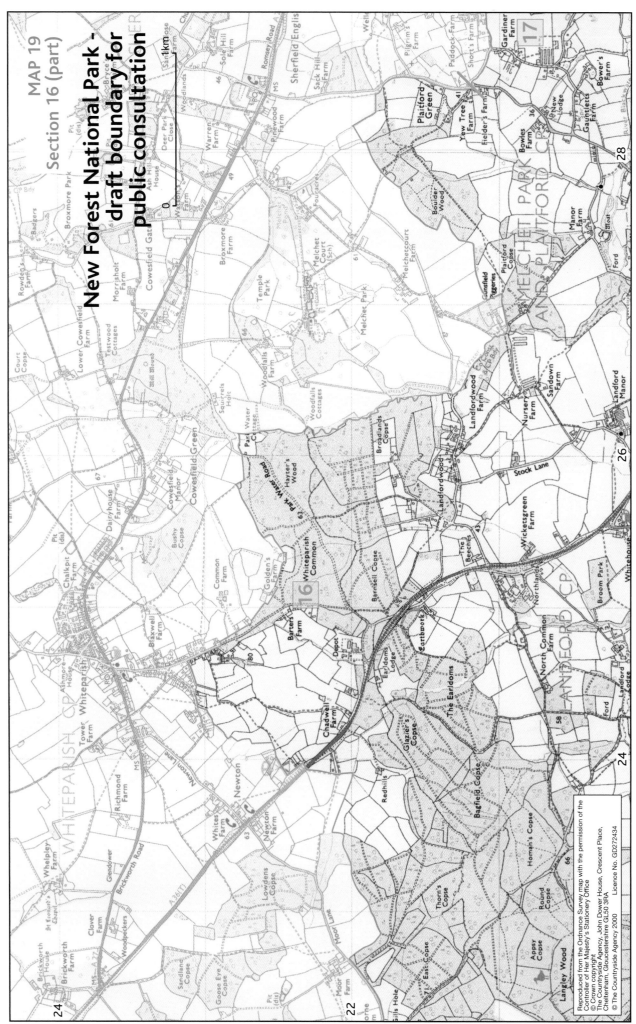

MAP 19
Section 16 (part)

**New Forest National Park -
draft boundary for
public consultation**

Scale 1km

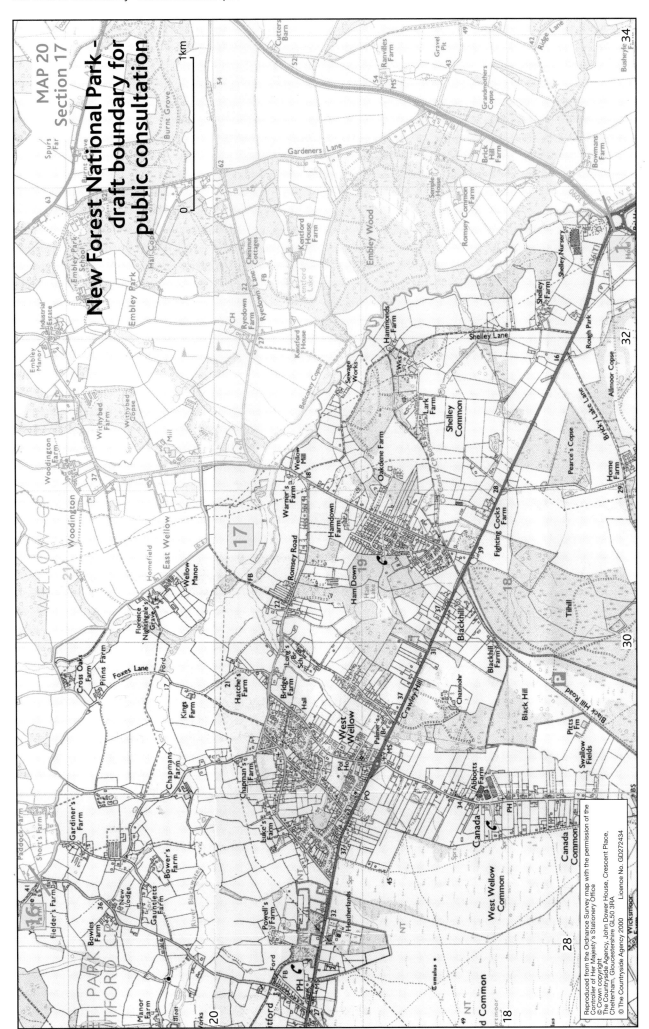

MAP 20
Section 17

New Forest National Park –
draft boundary for
public consultation